ROUTLEDGE LIBRARY EDITIONS:
INDUSTRIAL ECONOMICS

Volume 7

FIRM DIVERSIFICATION, MUTUAL FORBEARANCE BEHAVIOR AND PRICE-COST MARGINS

FIRM DIVERSIFICATION, MUTUAL FORBEARANCE BEHAVIOR AND PRICE-COST MARGINS

ALLYN D. STRICKLAND

Routledge
Taylor & Francis Group

LONDON AND NEW YORK

First published in 1984 by Garland Publishing, Inc.

This edition first published in 2018
by Routledge
2 Park Square, Milton Park, Abingdon, Oxon OX14 4RN

and by Routledge
711 Third Avenue, New York, NY 10017

Routledge is an imprint of the Taylor & Francis Group, an informa business

British Library Cataloguing in Publication Data
A catalogue record for this book is available from the British Library

ISBN: 978-1-138-30830-5 (Set)
ISBN: 978-1-351-21102-4 (Set) (ebk)
ISBN: 978-1-138-57069-6 (Volume 7) (hbk)
ISBN: 978-0-203-70332-8 (Volume 7) (ebk)

Publisher's Note
The publisher has gone to great lengths to ensure the quality of this reprint but points out that some imperfections in the original copies may be apparent.

Disclaimer
The publisher has made every effort to trace copyright holders and would welcome correspondence from those they have been unable to trace.

Firm Diversification, Mutual Forbearance Behavior and Price-Cost Margins

Allyn D. Strickland

Garland Publishing, Inc.
New York & London, 1984

Library of Congress Cataloging in Publication Data

Strickland, Allyn D.
    Firm diversification, mutual forbearance behavior and
price-cost margins.

    (Outstanding dissertations in economics)
    Originally presented as the author's thesis, University of
Wisconsin-Madison, 1976.
    Bibliography: p.
    1. Conglomerate corporations—United
States.   2. Competition—United States.
3. Diversification in industry—United States.   I. Title.
II. Title: Mutual forbearance behavior and price-cost
margins.   III. Series.
HD2756.U5S76   1984   338.8'3'0973   79-53209
ISBN 0-8240-4159-3

All volumes in this series are printed on acid-free,
250-year-life paper.

Printed in the United States of America

Public concern over conglomerate mergers has increased dramatically since this thesis was completed in August 1976. An accelera-
tion in conglomerate merger activity has rekindled firms' takeover
fears and swamped trustbusters in a scene reminiscent of the conglomerate merger wave of the 1960s. Attention has once again focused
on the political and economic issues surrounding conglomerate mergers,
especially those involving large firms. Of particular importance is
the possibility that conglomerate mergers may increase aggregate
concentration and eventually create an American "Zaibatsu" economy.

This thesis addressed this issue by examining Corwin Edwards'
mutual forbearance hypothesis. More specifically, do multi-market
contacts among diversified firms affect market competition? An
analysis of the manufacturing operations of 195 of the top 200
corporations in 1963 found many multi-market contacts, though they
did not lessen competition in the markets involved. These quantitative results suggest that anecdotal evidence of mutual forbearance
behavior substantially overstates the problem and that conglomerate
mergers should not be proscribed on this basis.

The limited empirical evidence on this issue has recently been
expanded by a study of mutual forbearance behavior in a regulated
sector (Review of Economics and Statistics, November 1978). Using a
methodological approach similar to that employed in this thesis,
Arnold Heggestad and Stephen Rhoades obtained indirect evidence that

multi-market contacts lessen competition in local banking markets.
It seems very likely, however, that their findings are relevant only
for the banking industry and cannot be applied to the manufacturing
sector of the economy. As Heggestad and Rhoades noted, the local
banking industry is "characterized by firms with relatively homogeneous product mixes" and firm diversification is "simply geographic
market extension rather than purely conglomerate." This market
environment is dramatically different from the heterogeneous world of
manufacturing where diversified firms have both horizontal and vertica
relationships involving numerous products across different industries.
For example, an average sample firm in the thesis had horizontal
contacts with 76 different firms and vertical contacts with all 194
sample firms. And the number of potential interfirm contacts has
undoubtedly increased since 1963.

In sum, mutual forbearance behavior does not seem feasible in
the complex, and increasingly international, business climate of leadi
domestic corporations. If it occurs at all, it will presumably be
isolated and limited to unique areas such as banking. This conclusion
removes one more potential economic argument against conglomerate
mergers and makes it increasingly likely that these mergers can only
be prohibited on political grounds. Indeed, there have been several
proposals (e.g., The Small and Independent Business Protection Act of
1979) to prohibit all large conglomerate mergers, thereby eliminating
the traditional economic requirement for an anticompetitive showing.

FIRM DIVERSIFICATION, MUTUAL FORBEARANCE BEHAVIOR

AND PRICE-COST MARGINS

by

ALLYN DOUGLAS STRICKLAND

A thesis submitted in partial fulfillment of the

requirements for the degree of

DOCTOR OF PHILOSOPHY

(Economics-Industrial Organization)

at the

UNIVERSITY OF WISCONSIN-MADISON

1976

To William F. Long and Leonard W. Weiss

ACKNOWLEDGMENTS

The author has received considerable guidance and support from several people. My major advisor, Leonard Weiss, contributed substantially to the development of my thesis as well as my skills as an economist. The other members of my committee, Frank Gollop and Willard Mueller, frequently provided helpful criticisms and sound advice. Frank Gollop was particularly instrumental in motivating the theoretical parts of my thesis. Finally, any acknowledgments on my part would be incomplete without thanking Bill and Jo Greene. Bill spent considerable time improving my programming skills, while Jo typed both drafts and my thesis. They also provided moral support and encouragement when they were most needed.

TABLE OF CONTENTS

LIST OF TABLES

CHAPTER I

Introduction

The American economy has experienced three major merger waves
in the last century. Although different in character, each merger
wave has had a substantial impact on the structure of American industry. The first merger wave, from approximately 1897 to 1904,
was characterized by mergers designed to monopolize entire industries.
Traditional giants such as United States Steel and International
Harvestor achieved dominance in their primary industries in
this fashion. The second major merger wave lasted from 1916 to
1929, ending with the stock market crash and the ensuing depression.
Many public utility and bank holding companies were created during
this period, which also saw an erosion in the market power of
monopolists. Mergers among second echelon firms transformed industries such as cement, tin cans, steel and agricultural implements
from near-monopolies to oligopolies [Markham (1955), Stigler (1968)].

The final, and most recent, major merger wave began around 1950
and steadily increased in intensity until 1969. This merger wave
surpassed the others in both numbers of mergers and in acquired
assets [F.T.C. (1969, p. 37)]. It was called the "conglomerate" merger wave due to the high proportion of mergers that were classified as
conglomerate. This historical trend toward conglomerate mergers
and away from horizontal and vertical mergers is illustrated in
Table I. Conglomerate mergers as a percent of total mergers increased from 19.3% during the late 1920's to 81.6% from 1966-1968.

During this same period, horizontal mergers decreased from 67.6% to 7.7%, while vertical mergers increased their share of total mergers from 4.8% to 9.8%.

The conglomerate merger wave was also distinguished by the magnitude of many of the mergers undertaken. Large corporations were routinely acquired by relatively unknown, fast-growing conglomerates. In 1968, 201 firms with assets in excess of $10 million each left the corporate scene through the merger route [F.T.C. (1969, p. 43)].

TABLE I

Percentage Distribution of Mergers by Type and Period,
1926-1968

	1926-1930	1940-1947	1951-1955	1956-1960	1961-1965	1966-1968
Horizontal	67.6	----	35.1	22.7	16.4	7.7
Market-Extension	8.3	----	4.1	7.4	6.1	0.9
SUBTOTAL	75.9	62.0	39.2	30.1	22.5	8.6
Vertical	4.8	17.0	12.2	14.9	17.5	9.8
Product-Extension and Other*	19.3	21.0	48.6	55.0	60.0	81.6
TOTAL	100.0	100.0	100.0	100.0	100.0	100.0

*   This category includes "pure" conglomerate mergers -- mergers in which there is no production or distribution relationship between the products of the acquired and acquiring firms.

SOURCE: U.S. Federal Trade Commission Economic Report on Corporate Mergers, Government Printing Office, Washington, D.C., 1969, p. 63.

These large acquisitons enabled firms like LTV and Gulf & Western
to climb from outside the top 200 manufacturing corporations in
1960 to positions within the top 50 in 1968 (22nd and 34th respectively). This change in the composition of the leading manufacturing
firms is illustrated in Table II which summarizes the merger activity
of the 25 most active acquiring firms from 1961-1968.

This substantial increase in conglomerate merger activity
created apprehension among both antitrust officials and academic
economists who were unsure of the competitive consequences of firm
diversification or "conglomeration." "Conglomeration" was hypothesized to have adverse consequences for the entire economy as well
as individual industries [Edwards (1955), Mueller (1969)]. At the
national level, it was feared that conglomeration would concentrate
economic power in fewer and fewer decision centers. Economists concerned with this issue have examined the historical trend in the percentage of manufacturing assets controlled by the top 200 corporations. As Table III indicates the trend has been toward increased
concentration, though the economic implications of this trend are
not readily apparent. Given the current state of economic theory,
this issue appears to be more political than economic. Throughout
American economic history, the public has associated large corporations with anti-competitive business practices, while enshrining the
small businessman as the guardian of our free enterprise system.

At the industry level, conglomerate mergers were hypothesized
to add an extra dimension to the elements of market structure and

TABLE II

ASSETS ACQUIRED BY 25 MOST ACTIVE ACQUIRING COMPANIES AMONG THE
200 LARGEST[1] MANUFACTURING CORPORATIONS, 1961-1968

Company	Acquisitions 1961-1968		Rank among largest industrial companies	
	Number	Total assets of acquired companies	1960	1968
Gulf & Western Industries, Inc.	67	$2,882	--	34
Ling-Temco-Vought, Inc.	23	1,901	335	22
International Telephone & Telegraph Corp.	47	1,487	35	15
Tenneco, Inc.	31	1,196	--	16
Teledyne, Inc.	125	1,026	--	136
McDonnell Douglas Corp.	8	864	242	62
Union Oil Company of Cal.	11	825	56	30
Sun Oil Company	3	808	54	28
Signal Companies, Inc.	10	770	126	66
Occidental Petroleum Corp.	15	767	--	41
Continental Oil Co.	19	686	45	24
General Telephone & Electronics Corp.	40	679	13	9
U.S. Plywood-Champion Papers, Inc.	27	649	176	74
Litton Industries, Inc.	79	609	275	67
Atlantic Richfield Co.	9	543	46	25
North American Rockwell Corp.	6	534	103	58
FMC Corp.	13	497	121	89
Studebaker-Worthington, Inc.	13	480	222	138
General American Transportation Corp.	4	453	94	123
Textron, Inc.	50	453	132	98
White Consolidated Industries, Inc.	28	443	--	133
Phillips Petroleum Co.	11	440	17	20
Colt Industries, Inc.	9	437	238	140
Radio Corp. of America	2	402	47	27
Georgia-Pacific Corp.	45	396	128	64
Total 25 companies	695	20,227		

[1] Ranks refer to FTC 200 largest manufacturing companies, except where noted, by asset size.

SOURCE: U.S. Federal Trade Commission <u>Economic Report on Corporate Mergers</u>, Government Printing Office, Washington, D.C., 1969, pp. 260-261.

TABLE III

SHARE OF MANUFACTURING ASSETS HELD BY THE 200 LARGEST

CORPORATIONS, 1925-41; 1947-68

| Year | Share held by 100 largest[1] | | Share held by 200 largest[1] | |
	Total assets	Corporate assets	Total assets	Corporate Ass.
1925	34.5	36.1		
1927	34.4	36.0		
1929	38.2	39.7	45.8	47.7
1931	41.7	43.4	49.0	50.9
1933	42.5	44.2	49.5	51.4
1935	40.8	42.3	47.7	49.6
1937	42.1	43.7	49.1	50.9
1939[2]	41.9	43.5	48.7	50.5
1941[2]	38.2	39.6	45.1	46.7
1947	37.5	39.3	45.0	47.2
1948	38.6	40.3	46.3	48.3
1949	39.5	41.1	47.1	49.0
1950	38.4	39.8	46.1	47.7
1951	38.1	39.4	46.1	47.7
1952	39.3	40.6	47.7	49.2
1953	40.3	41.7	48.7	50.3
1954	41.9	43.3	50.4	52.1
1955	43.0	44.3	51.6	53.1
1956	43.9	45.0	52.8	54.1
1957	45.2	46.3	54.3	55,6
1958	46.0	47.1	55.2	56.6
1959	45.4	46.3	54.8	56.0
1960	45.5	46.4	55.2	56.3
1961	45.8	46.6	55.4	56.3
1962	45.5	46.2	55.1	56.0
1963	45.7	46.5	55.5	56.3
1964	45.8	46.5	55.8	56.6
1965	45.9	46.5	55.9	56.7
1966	45.8	46.4	56.1	56.7
1967	47.6	48.1	58.7	59.3
1968	48.8	49.3	60.4	60.9
Percentage Point Increase				
1925-1968 14.3		13.2	----	----
1947-1968 11.3		10.0	15.4	13.7
Percent Increase in Share				
1925-1968 41.4		36.6	----	----
1947-1968 30.1		25.4	34.2	29.0

[1] Ranked according to asset size in each year.

[2] Data are not available for the years between 1941 and 1947 because some large corporations did not publish balance sheets for reasons of wartime security.

SOURCE: U.S. Federal Trade Commission Economic Report on Corporate Mergers, Government Printing Office, Washington, D.C., 1969, p. 173.

behavior analyzed in traditional models of the theory of the firm [Edwards (1955)]. In particular, conglomeration increases the likelihood of a firm engaging in reciprocity, cross-subsidization, and/or mutual forbearance behavior. If these practices are anti-competitive, competition in an industry may be reduced as the industry's firms become more and more conglomerate in character.

This thesis will focus on the mutual forbearance behavior hypothesized to be a function of firm conglomeration. The thesis will examine the hypothesis in the context of firm diversification though, since mutual forbearance behavior may result from firm contacts created by vertical and horizontal, as well as conglomerate, acquisitions. The hypothesized anticompetitive consequences of conglomeration are, in actuality, a subset of those associated with diversification in general.

Historically the mutual forbearance hypothesis was first enunciated by Corwin Edwards in 1955, over a decade before the conglomerate merger wave became a major concern of economists. He maintained that:

> When one large conglomerate enterprise competes with another, the two are likely to encounter each other in a considerable number of markets. The multiplicity of their contacts may blunt the edge of their competition....Each may informally recognize the other's primacy of interest in markets important to the other, in the expectation that its own important interests will be similarly respected [Edwards (1955, p. 335)].

This argument drops the traditional assumption of market independence by asserting that firm profit maximization requires an awareness of

rivals, and their interactions, <u>across</u> markets. Firms will recognize
each other's "spheres of influence" by adopting non-aggressive behavior in those markets for fear of retaliation in other markets.
This hypothesis thus implies that behavior in one market is conditioned by contacts in other markets.

The crucial step in the creation of mutual forbearance behavior
is firm diversification. Through diversification a firm increases
the number of its contacts with other firms throughout the economy.
These contacts create an awareness among those firms of their common,
multi-market interests. Firms recognize that their interdependence
is not limited to any single market. This recognition of interdependence will lead those firms to adopt mutual forbearance policies
in those markets where they interact. Competition will thus be less
than if each firm independently pursued a policy of profit maximization. In this fashion, increased diversification, either through
internal growth or outside acquisitions, increases the likelihood
of mutual forbearance behavior.

From a public policy perspective, such behavior poses difficult
problems for the Justice Department and Federal Trade Commission.
The successful prosecution of Section 7 merger cases requires a
showing that there may be a substantial lessening of competition
"in any line of commerce in any part of the country." With mutual
forbearance behavior, however, it is possible that a proposed merger
would not violate Justice Department guidelines or current case
law, but would reduce competition in many markets. A substantial

lessening of competition may be shown, but not necessarily in the market involving the merger.

The different aspects of mutual forbearance behavior, and their implications for competition, are illustrated by the Consolidated Foods case. Consolidated Foods was a large food manufacturer with some retail operations. In 1965 it entered the Chicago retail market by acquiring 7 Eagle Food Stores and immediately initiating an aggressive price campaign. This action was resented by National Tea, the nation's fourth largest food chain with 237 stores in the Chicago area. In response, National Tea ordered its stores not to buy Sarah Lee bakery products, which were produced by Consolidated, for one week. At the company's annual meeting, National Tea's president had commented that a "large competitor who is also a manufacturer, has come out and murdered prices...and sold so many items below costs" that the firm had been warned: "Tomorrow there will be fewer of your lines on our shelves" [F.T.C. (1969, p. 46)]. Shortly thereafter, Eagle Foods discontinued their aggressive pricing policy and were subsequently sold by Consolidated, who left the Chicago market. According to Consolidated's president:

> We have now concluded that it would be advisable from the standpoint of operating efficiency to withdraw from Chicago and confine our activities to those sections of Iowa, Wisconsin, Illinois, and Minnesota in which our Supermarket business has been historically operated [F.T.C. (1969, p. 469)].

The Consolidated Foods case illustrates how mutual forbearance behavior may affect firm conduct and, therefore, industry conduct and performance. First of all, pricing policies may be less aggressive where recognized interdependence among multi-market firms is substantial. Interdependence from multi-market contacts may strengthen oligopolistic interdependence in a single market, thereby increasing the likelihood of firms adopting a policy of joint profit maximization. Secondly, multi-market interdependence may affect a firm's entry decisions. Large, diversified firms may only enter industries where "conflicts" with other large, diversified firms would be minimized. Alternatively, they might enter industries where these contacts would be substantial in order to gain leverage over their multi-market competitors. Thirdly, if multi-market interdependence does inhibit price competition, it may lead to an increase in non-price competition. Firms might increase their expenditures on advertising and possibly even research and development as alternative means of competing for market shares. Alternatively, strong interdependence may reduce competition in non-price areas although this seems less likely given the unpredictable payoffs and long lead times associated with those activities. In sum, firm diversification may adversely affect several dimensions of industry conduct through the creation of mutual forbearance behavior among an industry's firms.

Since the conglomerate merger wave, interest in the anti-competitive aspects of conglomerate mergers has diminished. The few empirical studies in this area have examined the effect of conglomerate mergers on industry concentration [Goldberger (1974), Markham (1973), F.T.C. (1969), F.T.C. (1972)] and the incidence of reciprocity among leading firms [Allen (1975)]. No studies have dealt with the relationship between firm diversification and mutual forbearance behavior. Consequently there is no evidence on the prevalence of this particular activity in the American economy. It is not possible to tell if the cases which have been found constitute the entire problem or are merely the tip of the iceberg.

One major objective of this thesis is the quantification of the number and magnitude of interfirm contacts among the leading firms in the manufacturing sector of the American economy. These firms may interact in both horizontal and vertical capacities. Two firms have a horizontal relationship whenever they meet as competitors. This information can be obtained from Fortune's Plant and Product Directory which lists every four-digit manufacturing S.I.C. in which a top 1,000 firm (based on annual sales) was active during 1963-1964. This time period was chosen since 1963 was a Census year and industry data is therefore available from the Census of Manufactures.

Vertical relationships exist between two firms when they interact in buyer and/or seller capacities. This information is more difficult to obtain as it requires detailed information about a firm's customers and suppliers. Such an undertaking requires resources beyond those available to the author. The 1963 input-output tables published by the Office of Business Economics will be used instead to determine "potential" vertical relationships between firms. The word "potential" is emphasized since a vertical relationship may exist between two industries, but not necessarily between two specific firms in those industries. In the fashion outlined above, it will be possible to capture the actual horizontal and potential vertical relationships for a sample of leading firms.

The second major objective of this thesis is to conduct a specific test for one aspect of mutual forbearance behavior. As noted above, the mutual forbearance hypothesis asserts that external contacts increase firm interdependence, thereby lessening competition among an industry's firms. One implication of this is that it should be easier for diversified firms to attain and maintain a policy of joint, as opposed to individual, profit maximization. The greater perceived interdependence among diversified firms should facilitate the adoption of covert and/or overt measures designed to lessen, if not altogether eliminate, price competition. This point was stressed by the Federal Trade Commission in their Economic Report on Corporate Mergers.

> The simplest form of conglomerate interdependence probably
> involves pricing decisions. Firms that meet as competitors
> in many markets are likely to regard each other with greater
> deference than if their decisions were constrained solely
> by what happened in a particular market. The resulting
> mutual forbearance in making pricing decisions results,
> because conglomerate rivals may hesitate to gain an advan-
> tage in one market by price cutting lest their conglomerate
> rivals retaliate in others. This is illustrated by the
> great deference other food chains have traditionally shown
> the Great Atlantic and Pacific Tea Company (A&P) which,
> as the Nation's largest food chain, operates in over 1,000
> different communities [F.T.C. (1969, p. 46)].

The mutual forbearance hypothesis thus predicts a positive relationship between industry profitability and firm interdependence arising
from external contacts.

This thesis will empirically test this hypothesized relationship
for industries in the manufacturing sector of the American economy.
Indices of firm interdependence will be constructed and used in
cross-section analyses of the determinants of industry price-cost
margins. These indices will capture all horizontal and vertical
relationships of an industry's firms. In this fashion it will be
possible to subject to empirical analysis this dimension of mutual
forbearance behavior.

CHAPTER II

Multi-Market Contacts, Firm Interdependence

and Industry Profitability

Traditional analyses of the theory of the firm emphasize the
importance of the number of sellers in determining market conduct
and performance [Fellner (1949]. It has been hypothesized that
firm interdependence increases as the number of sellers decreases,
thereby facilitating the adoption of joint profit-maximizing
policies [Chamberlin (1956)]. The mutual forbearance hypothesis
asserts that firm interdependence in one market can be strengthened
by firms' contacts outside that market. Hence, price competition
in one market can be modified by contacts in other markets
[Edwards (1955), Mueller (1969)]. This chapter provides a framework
for analyzing and empirically testing this dimension of mutual
forbearance behavior.

I. Single-Market Models

In a competitive market a firm makes output decisions independently of, and without consideration for, its competitors. A firm
maximizes profits by simply expanding output until its marginal
cost equals the prevailing market price (assuming that the second-
order conditions for a profit maximum are satisfied). Since there
are many sellers, no single seller can influence market price and,
hence indirectly, the output decisions of its competitors. As a
result, there is no interdependence among firms in a competitive

market.

This situation does not hold in oligopolistic markets where firms are price makers, not price takers. A change in one firm's output level can affect industry price and the profit-maximizing output levels of its competitors. When an oligopolist changes its output, it _must_ consider both the direct and indirect consequences of that change. Fewness of sellers thus creates a "recognized interdependence" among those sellers [Chamberlin (1956)]. The exact nature of that interdependence is specified by the firms' reaction functions [Fellner (1949), Iwata (1974)].

In oligopolistic markets, therefore, a firm's conduct will be conditioned by its perceived interdependence with its competitors. Of particular interest is the expected effect of firm inter-dependence on market price. Chamberlin argues that fewness of sellers will lead to monopoly pricing [Chamberlin (1956)].

> If each seeks his maximum profit rationally and intelli-
> gently, he will realize that when there are only two or
> a few sellers his own move has a considerable effect
> upon his competitors, and that this makes it idle to
> suppose that they will accept without retaliation the
> losses he forces upon them. Since the result of a cut
> by any one is inevitably to decrease his own profits, no
> one will cut, and although the sellers are entirely
> independent, the equilibrium result is the same as
> though there were a monopolistic agreement between them.
> [Chamberlin (1956), p. 48].

Recognition of interdependence leads to recognition of joint inter-ests -- the desire to maximize profits -- and the means to do so -- independent monopoly pricing.

Chamberlin's oligopoly model predicts that firms can adopt a joint profit-maximizing policy without colluding. A monopoly pricing scheme naturally follows from their recognition of joint interests. In reality this is unlikely to happen. The main stumbling block is the determination of "the" monopoly price which maximizes firm profits. When firms have different cost structures, perceptions of the elasticity of their demand curve, and/or future expectations, they will disagree over the appropriate monopoly price [Scherer (1970)]. Without some collusive arrangement, price will either be set by the low-cost firm or through competitive pressures should disagreement end in price warfare.

The ability to attain a collusive agreement, whether covert or overt, should increase with a decrease in the number of sellers [Scherer (1970)]. With fewer firms, there are fewer independent decision centers which must be contacted in order to reach an agreement. Also, as the number of firms decreases, so does the likelihood that one of them will be a maverick and oppose any collective decision.

The ability to preserve a collusive agreement also depends on the number of firms. Once, a collusive agreement is reached, there is a strong temptation to cheat on the agreement and expand sales at less than the collusive price. The likelihood of cheating depends on the magnitude of the benefits and the probability of being detected. Stigler has shown that the probability of detection increases as the number of firms decreases, where detection depends on a firm experiencing significant increases in sales [Stigler (1968)].

In sum, the ability to attain and maintain collusive agreements are both negatively related to the number of firms in a market. This suggests an inverse relationship between number of sellers and market profitability. The most frequently used proxy for number of sellers has been the four-firm concentration ratio -- the percentage of industry value of shipments shipped by the industry's four largest firms. As concentration increases, so does firm interdependence and the likelihood of collusion.

II. Multi-Market Models

Most oligopoly models analyze firms which are active in only one market [Fellner (1949)]. When a multi-market firm is assumed, it maximizes total profits by simply maximizing profits in each of its markets [Henderson and Quandt (1971)]. Assuming that the markets are not vertically related, a firm's decisions in one market are made independently of those in its other markets. A multi-market firm will not behave any differently than its single-market competitors.

This model may be inappropriate for diversified firms which meet as competitors or buyers-sellers in many markets. Among such firms, a policy designed specifically for one market may provoke retaliation by its competitors across many markets. A multi-market firm must also evaluate the direct and indirect effects of its actions, but the indirect effects may no longer be confined to just a single market. In sum, if a market's firms are diversified, firm interdependence may be a function of their relationships both inside and outside that market.

This suggests that diversified firms which meet in many markets may have a greater perceived interdependence than single-market firms. This point is illustrated by a hypothetical example of Adams [Adams (1974)].

> Suppose a firm sells in ten distinct markets with a share of ten percent in each. Suppose, further, that in every one of these markets, the firm has nine competitors, each also with a ten percent share. If the nine competitors in any one market have no positions in the other nine markets, the original firm has a total of ninety competitors. If however, the nine competitors in any one market also have positions in each of the other nine markets, the original firm has a total of only nine competitors. While the intramarket fewness of sellers in these two examples is identical, the likelihood that sellers will recognize their interdependence in any given market is substantially greater in the latter case. [Adams (1974), p. 1282].

Firm interdependence from intra-market contacts may be supplemented by firm interdependence arising from substantial multi-market contacts.

The crucial issue is whether or not firm interdependence from external contacts increases the ability of firms in any single market to attain and maintain a collusive arrangement, whether it be overt or covert in nature. The mutual forbearance hypothesis asserts that firm interdependence arising from multi-market contacts does lessen competition among a market's firms [Edwards (1955)]. Each firm adopts a mutual forbearance stance and respects the others' "spheres of influence" in the expectation that they will do the same. This point has been stressed by

Mueller [Mueller (1969)].

> Conglomeration, by increasing both size and diversification, increases the number of contact points shared with competitors, suppliers, and customers, thereby increasing the mutual awareness of common interests among firms that share points of contact.
>
> The simplest form of conglomerate interdependence probably involves pricing decisions. Firms that meet as competitors in many markets are likely to regard one another with greater deference than if their decisions were constrained solely by what happened in a particular market. The resulting mutual forbearance in making pricing decisions results because conglomerate rivals are less likely to push their advantage in one market lest their conglomerate rivals retaliate in others. [Mueller (1969), p. 1492]

A similar argument is made by Adams who believes that multi-market contacts increase "the likelihood of collusion...by simplifying the coordination machinery required to maintain collusive agreements" [Adams (1974, p. 1283)]. Firms can spread the benefits of collusion across markets via increased market shares for participating firms instead of relying on side payments in any single market. He also argues that the probability of cheating on a collusive agreement is less among multi-market firms since "cheating in any one market is more likely to be detected when all participating firms interact in the same economically related markets" [Adams (1974, p. 1284)].

The importance of firm interdependence from intra- and inter-market contacts can also be analyzed with duopoly models. (See the appendix to this chapter.) This simply requires using conjectural variation functions to capture a duopolist's perceived multi-market interdependence with its competitor. When this is done, both intra- and inter-market interdependence operate to reduce the profit-maximizing output level of the firm. Each type of interdependence has an independent effect and reduces a duopolist's output level below that of a Cournot duopolist who assumes no interdependence with its competitor.

The above arguments support the ability of diversified firms to create collusive agreements across the markets in which they interact. The major selling point is the potentially large costs imposed upon a cheater across many markets in retaliation for a sin committed in one. There are, however, two considerations which argue against the likelihood of multi-market collusion among diversified firms.

First, as noted in the section on single-market models, there are obstacles to collusive agreements among firms. Firms with different cost structures, perceptions of industry elasticity of demand, and future expectations must agree on the appropriate price which will maximize joint profits. This difficulty will be compounded the more differentiated the market's product [Scherer (1970)]. If the probability of a market's firms agreeing on a collusive price is p, the probability of reaching such agreements in n markets is p^n. Even if multi-market contacts _increase_ the probability of reaching an agreement in a single market, the probability of obtaining multi-market collusive agreements still diminishes with increases in the number of markets.

Secondly, the mutual forbearance hypothesis implicitly assumes

that pricing decisions of diversified firms are centralized
decisions. Top management is aware of the myriad relationships
it has with its diversified competitors and orchestrates the
agreements necessary for multi-market collusion. If firms are
organized on a divisional or profit-center basis, however, pricing
decisions may be decentralized [Williamson and Bhargava (1972)].
In that case, the manager of one division may only be concerned
with the performance of his division and not with the welfare of
other divisions. This situation would not be conducive to multi-
market agreements, especially if such agreements were not in the
interests of all managers.

Those two qualifications suggest an alternative hypothesis
to the mutual forbearance hypothesis -- an increase in external
contacts among firms does not increase the ability of those firms to
attain and maintain collusive agreements. The question thus becomes
an empirical one. In the last section in this chapter measures
of firm interdependence are derived which capture the multi-market
aspect of firm contacts. These measures are then used as additional
explanatory variables in a cross-section analysis of the determinants
of industry price-cost margins. In this manner it is possible
to capture the influence of firm interdependence arising from both
intra- and inter-market contacts among an industry's firms.

III. Measures of Firm Interdependence

There are obviously many factors which can create perceived
interdependence among firms. Such institutional arrangements as

joint ventures, trade associations, patent pools and "Judge Gary"
dinners immediately come to mind. The mutual forbearance hypothesis,
however, asserts that perceived interdependence among firms is
created by multi-market contacts. A firm tempers its aggressive
behavior in one market for fear of its rivals' retaliation in other
markets. The potential gains from aggressive action in one industry
may be offset, or even exceeded, by losses from other markets in
which it produces. This analysis thus assumes that a firm will
restrain its aggressive behavior if it is inconsistent with profit
maximization.

The above considerations imply that a firm's perceived interdependence with a competitor will be greater, ceteris paribus, the
greater is the competitor's ability to inflict "financial punishment."
This approach is consistent with game theoretic models of market
behavior where firms are considered combatants in a game of economic
survival [Shubik (1960)]. In that context, firm recognition is a
function of the potentially adverse strategy options available to
competitors. A firm recognizes its interdependence with those
firms which have the potential for interfering with its goal of
maximizing profits.

This last point has long been stressed in traditional models
of the theory of the firm. A major characteristic used in classifying markets has been the sensitivity of one firm's profits with
respect to an output change by a competitor.

An oligopolistic industry contains a number sufficiently small so that the actions of any individual seller have a perceptible influence upon his rivals. It is not sufficient to distinguish oligopoly from perfect competition for a homogeneous product or from the many-sellers case of monopolistic competition for a differentiated product on the basis of the number of sellers alone. The essential distinguishing feature is the interdependence of the various sellers' actions. If the influence of one seller's quantity decision upon the profit of another, $\partial \Pi_i / \partial Q_j$ is imperceptible, the industry satisfies the basic requirement for either perfect competition or the many-sellers case of monopolistic competition. If $\partial \Pi_i / \partial Q_j$ is of a noticeable order of magnitude, it is duopolistic or oligopolistic. [Henderson and Quandt (1971, p. 222)].

This thesis will adopt this "profit sensitivity" criterion in constructing measures of firm interdependence. This decision does not imply that other factors such as institutional environment are not important in creating firm interdependence. It does assume, however, that these factors are of secondary importance compared to the "profit sensitivity" criterion.

Martin Shubik has suggested using "short-run market vulnerability" as a measure of firm interdependence [Shubik (1960)]. He defines this measure as "the amount of damage that can be done to a firm by a short-run market action of an opponent or by a shift in a market parameter." [Shubik (1960, p. 293)] This measure can be illustrated using a simple example of two firms (A and B).

In a quantity variation model, Shubik's measure of firm A's interdependence with B is simply the differential of A's profits with respect to a change in B's output level.

(1) $\qquad dΠ_A = \dfrac{\partial\ Π_A}{\partial\ Q_B} \cdot d\ Q_B$

In this general case, A's interdependence with B is a function of
both the marginal impact of a unit change by B ($\partial\ Π_A/\partial\ Q_B$) and
the absolute amount of that change (dQ_B). As both of these increase,
ceteris paribus, so will the incremental change in A's profits and
therefore its perceived interdependence with B.

Shubik's measure can be misleading, however, for it deals in
absolute and not relative terms. Depending on firm size a potential
loss of $10 million could be considered disastrous or mildly dis-
comforting. This deficiency can be eliminated by dividing (1) by
firm A's total profits, thereby making the measure a relative one.

(2) $\qquad \dfrac{dΠ_A}{Π_A} = \dfrac{\partial\ Π_A}{\partial\ Q_B} \cdot \dfrac{dQ_B}{Π_A}$

This modification improves Shubik's measure but it too has a
serious flaw. All of the above measures indicate the change in A's
profits with respect to changes in B's output levels, but B's
changes are in absolute terms. B's ability to "flood the market"
with 100 additional units of Q_B, for example will depend on B's
total production of Q_B. If Q_B is currently 10,000, then 100
additional units could presumably be produced with little extra
effort. But, if current production is 100, an expansion of that
magnitude would require construction of a new plant which is not
possible in the short run.

This problem can be solved by multiplying the right side of (2) by a well-chosen one (Q_B/Q_B)

$$\frac{d\Pi_A}{\Pi_A} = \frac{\partial \Pi_A}{\partial Q_B} \cdot \frac{dQ_B}{\Pi_A} \cdot \frac{Q_B}{Q_B}$$

and then rearranging terms to express the percentage change in A's profits as

$$(3) \qquad \frac{d\Pi_A}{\Pi_A} = \frac{\partial \Pi_A}{\partial Q_B} \cdot \frac{Q_B}{\Pi_A} \cdot \frac{dQ_B}{Q_B}$$

Dividing both sides by the percentage change in B's output then transforms Shubik's original absolute measure of interdependence into an elasticity measure of interdependence.

$$(4) \qquad \eta_{\Pi_A,Q_B} = \frac{\partial \Pi_A}{\partial Q_B} \cdot \frac{Q_B}{\Pi_A}$$

All we have done in steps (2) through (4) is to provide a rationale for defining the criterion for firm interdependence in terms of the elasticity of A's profits with respect to an output change by B.

This "elasticity" measure of firm interdependence does have many desirable properties. First, it applies whether A and B interact in a single market or in n different markets. Thus, it captures all inter-market contacts and, hence, potential areas of retaliation among firms. The total elasticity is simply a weighted average of the different market elasticities.[1] Secondly, since it is an elasticity measure, it deals with relative, not absolute, profit and output changes. Thirdly, the measure is not necessarily symmetric. Firm A's perceived interdependence with firm B may equal B's perceived interdependence with A, but it is not constrained to do so by the measure itself. Fourthly, the profit-elasticity measure is consistent with the "profit sensitivity" criterion discussed above.

This general measure of firm interdependence will now be applied to the actual relationships which can exist between firms. Since firms can interact in both horizontal (direct competitiors) and vertical (buyer-seller) capacities, it is necessary to construct measures which reflect these different types of inter-firm relationships. Once these indices of horizontal and vertical firm interdependence have been derived, they will be aggregated into industry measures which can be used in cross-section analyses of the determinants of industry price-cost margins.

A. <u>Horizontal Interdependence</u>

A horizontal relationship exists between two firms when they meet as competitors in a given industry. Horizontal interdependence arises when those firms meet as competitors in two or more industries <u>and</u> those contacts in other industries affect their behavior toward each other in a single industry. The firm perceives the fortunes of the two industries to be interrelated.

Assume that two firms (A and B) are direct competitors in industry one. They produce differentiated products and therefore have their own demand curves. A's inverse demand curve can be expressed as

(1) $Q_{A1} = F_1(P_{A1})$

where Q_{A1} and P_{A1} are A's output level and price in market one. In addition, it is assumed that $\partial Q_{A1}/\partial P_{A1} < 0$ and $\partial P_{A1}/\partial Q_{B1} \leq 0$, indicating that A faces a downward-sloping demand curve which may be affected by B's output level.

A's profit level equals

(2) $\Pi_A = P_{A1}Q_{A1} - C_{A1}$

where C_{A1} is A's total production costs and is a function of the output level. It is also assumed that A picks that price-quantity combination which maximizes its profit given its demand curve.

The sensitivity of A's profits to an output change by B can be analyzed by taking the partial derivative of (2) with respect to Q_{B1}.

(3) $\dfrac{\partial \Pi_A}{\partial Q_{B1}} = Q_{A1}\dfrac{\partial P_{A1}}{\partial Q_{B1}} + P_{A1}\dfrac{\partial Q_{A1}}{\partial Q_{B1}} - C'_{A1}\dfrac{\partial Q_{A1}}{\partial Q_{B1}}$

Rearranging terms we have

$$(3') \quad \frac{\partial \Pi_A}{\partial Q_{B1}} = Q_{A1} \frac{\partial P_{A1}}{\partial Q_{B1}} + (P_{A1} - C'_{A1}) \frac{\partial Q_{A1}}{\partial Q_{B1}}$$

which indicates that an output change by B may change A's inital price-output combination.

The elasticity of A's profits with respect to output changes by B (n_{Π_A, Q_B}) can be derived in a straightforward manner. First, we multiply both sides of (3') by Q_{B1}/Π_A.

$$(4) \quad \frac{\partial \Pi_A}{\partial Q_{B1}} \cdot \frac{Q_{B1}}{\Pi_A} = Q_{A1} \frac{\partial P_{A1}}{\partial Q_{B1}} \cdot \frac{Q_{B1}}{\Pi_A} + (P_{A1} - C'_{A1}) \frac{\partial Q_{A1}}{\partial Q_{B1}} \cdot \frac{Q_{B1}}{\Pi_A}$$

Note that the left side of (4) can now be written as the profit elasticity -- n_{Π_A, Q_B}. And, through the application of the chain rule, the partial derivative of Q_{A1} with respect to Q_{B1} equals

$$\frac{\partial Q_{A1}}{\partial Q_{B1}} = \frac{\partial Q_{A1}}{\partial P_{A1}} \cdot \frac{\partial P_{A1}}{\partial Q_{B1}}$$

These changes are now substituted into (4).

$$(4') \quad n_{\Pi_A, Q_B} = Q_{A1} \frac{\partial P_{A1}}{\partial Q_{B1}} \cdot \frac{Q_{B1}}{\Pi_A} + (P_{A1} - C'_{A1}) \frac{\partial Q_{A1}}{\partial P_{A1}} \cdot \frac{\partial P_{A1}}{\partial Q_{B1}} \cdot \frac{Q_{B1}}{\Pi_A}$$

Next, both terms on the right side of (4') are multiplied by well-chosen ones (P_{A1}/P_{A1} for the first term and $(P_{A1}/P_{A1}) \cdot (Q_{A1}/Q_{A1})$ for the second).

$$\eta_{\Pi_A, Q_B} = Q_{A1} \frac{\partial P_{A1}}{\partial Q_{B1}} \cdot \frac{Q_{B1}}{\Pi_A} \cdot \frac{P_{A1}}{P_{A1}}$$

$$+ (P_{A1} - C'_{A1}) \frac{\partial Q_{A1}}{\partial P_{A1}} \cdot \frac{\partial P_{A1}}{\partial Q_{B1}} \cdot \frac{Q_{B1}}{\Pi_A} \cdot \frac{P_{A1}}{P_{A1}} \cdot \frac{Q_{A1}}{Q_{A1}} .$$

Rearranging terms we obtain the following

$$\eta_{\Pi_A, Q_B} = \frac{P_{A1} Q_{A1}}{\Pi_A} \left(\frac{\partial P_{A1}}{\partial Q_{B1}} \cdot \frac{Q_{B1}}{P_{A1}} \right)$$

$$+ \frac{(P_{A1} - C'_{A1}) Q_{A1}}{\Pi_A} \left(\frac{\partial Q_{A1}}{\partial P_{A1}} \cdot \frac{P_{A1}}{Q_{A1}} \right) \left(\frac{\partial P_{A1}}{\partial Q_{B1}} \cdot \frac{Q_{B1}}{P_{A1}} \right)$$

where the terms in brackets may now be written as elasticities.

(5) $$\eta_{\Pi_A, Q_B} = \frac{P_{A1} Q_{A1}}{\Pi_A} \cdot \eta_{P_{A1}, Q_{B1}}$$

$$+ \frac{(P_{A1} - C'_{A1}) Q_{A1}}{\Pi_A} \cdot \eta_{Q_{A1}, P_{A1}} \cdot \eta_{P_{A1}, Q_{B1}}$$

$\eta_{P_{A1}, Q_{B1}}$ is the elasticity of A's price with respect to B's output, while $\eta_{Q_{A1}, P_{A1}}$ is the elasticity of A's output with respect to its own price. Since the elasticity of A's price with respect to B's output appears in both terms it can be factored out, leaving the following expression for the elasticity of A's profits with respect to Q_{B1}.

$$
(6) \qquad \eta_{\Pi_A, Q_B} = \eta_{P_{A1}, Q_{B1}} \left[\frac{P_{A1} Q_{A1}}{\Pi_A} + \frac{(P_{A1} - C'_{A1}) Q_{A1}}{\Pi_A} \cdot \eta_{Q_{A1}, P_{A1}} \right]
$$

There are three main things to note about (6). First, the profit elasticity equals zero when the price elasticity is zero. This corresponds to the monopolistic competition case where one competitor cannot affect the market price and hence output level and profits of another competitor. In such a case, firm inter-dependence equals zero. Secondly, the effect of a price reduction on A's profits can be broken down into two components -- the price and output effects. The price effect -- the first term in the brackets -- indicates that the current value of sales $(P_{A1} Q_{A1})$ will decrease if P_{A1} decreases. A will receive a lower price per unit for its current output level. And since production costs for these units are unchanged, A's profits must decrease. Opposing the price effect is the output effect -- the second term in brackets. Since A has a downward sloping demand curve, a reduction in price may lead to an increase in output. The addition to A's profits will depend on the amount by which unit price exceeds unit marginal cost $(P_{A1} - C'_{A1})$ and the absolute increase in production. This last factor depends on the elasticity of A's demand curve. If A's demand curve is perfectly inelastic, there will not be an output effect. In sum, the elasticity of A's profits with respect to output variation by B is a function of both $\eta_{P_{A1}, Q_{B1}}$ and $\eta_{Q_{A1}, P_{A1}}$.

In this framework A is "passively" responding to a change in its market environment -- the position of its demand curve -- brought about by the action of a competitor. In Cournot fashion, firm A is merely moving to a new price-quantity combination given the new price. If A's profits are substantially affected by B's output change, it will be assumed that A recognizes its interdependence with B. If A's profits are not affected, however, interdependence does not exist. This "passive" measure of firm interdependence is thus consistent with the profit sensitivity criterion discussed above.

In empirically estimating (6), it is possible to estimate firm sales and price-cost margins at the industry level from four-digit Census data. Firm A's sales in market one and its margin on those sales is simply its market share multiplied by industry value of shipments and industry margins, respectively. Firm profits can be obtained, though they will vary among firms due to different accounting procedures and the extent of non-manufacturing and foreign operations. Two alternatives are available. Use either firm sales or firm margins as a substitute for total firm profits. As noted above, both of these figures can be estimated for the firm's domestic manufacturing operations, which is the area of analysis. Since firm margins is closer to firm profits in order of magnitude, it will be used as the proxy instead of firm sales. Another estimation problem concerns the two elasticities, $\eta_{P_{A1}, Q_{B1}}$ and $\eta_{Q_{A1}, P_{A1}}$; estimates of which are not available. The elasticity of A's price in market one with respect to B's output will be greater, <u>ceteris paribus</u>, the larger is B's market share in that market. Unfortunately, there is no comparable proxy for the elasticity of firm A's demand curve. As a result, (6) will be estimated using four different assumptions about the elasticity of the firm's demand curve: 0, $-\frac{1}{2}$, -1 and -2. It should be noted that as the firm's demand curve becomes more elastic, the output effect tends to counter the price effect, thereby reducing η_{Π_A, Q_B}.

A's perceived horizontal interdependence with B will then be defined as

$$(7) \qquad HI_{A,B} = MS_{B1} \left[\frac{S_{A1}}{M_A} + \frac{M_{A1}}{M_A} \cdot \eta_{Q_{A1}, P_{A1}} \right]$$

Where MS_{B1} is B's market share in market one, S_{A1} and M_{A1} are A's sales and margins on those sales in market one, and M_A is A's total margin from all of its manufacturing sales. As noted above, this measure will be estimated under four different assumptions about $\eta_{Q_{A1}, P_{A1}}$. Since the market share of B is a proxy for $\eta_{P_{A1}, Q_{B1}}$ it should have a negative sign. But, following the common practice of making elasticities positive, the measure is defined as a positive number by multiplying it by a minus one.

To obtain a measure of A's total horizontal interdependence with B when they compete across many industries, we sum (7) for all j industries in which A produces

$$(8) \quad HI_{AB} = \sum_j MS_{Bj} \left[\frac{S_{Aj}}{M_A} + \frac{M_{Aj}}{M_A} \cdot \eta_{Q_{Aj}, P_{Aj}} \right]$$

If B does not produce in the jth industry, MS_{Bj} will equal zero and that industry will not affect A's horizontal interdependence with B.

This approach can also be used to construct a measure of A's horizontal interdependence with all of its competitors in industry one. Firm A's behavior will be influenced by its perceived interdependence with all of its competitors, since any aggressive action by A will affect all of them. Summing (8) over firm A's m competitors in industry one gives us a measure reflecting the sensitivity of A's sales to actions taken by its competitors in that industry:

$$(9) \quad HI_{Am} = \sum_m \sum_j MS_{mj} \left[\frac{S_{Aj}}{M_A} + \frac{M_{Aj}}{M_A} \cdot \eta_{Q_{Aj}, P_{Aj}} \right]$$

It should be stressed that (9) is a measure of firm A's total horizontal interdependence with its competitors in industry one. As such, it includes horizontal interdependence arising from contacts both within and without that industry. In order to test the mutual forbearance hypothesis it is necessary to capture interdependence from external contacts only. Thus, when these measures are computed, they will not be summed over the industry of analysis (i.e., in this case $j \neq 1$).

B. Vertical Interdependence

A firm can have two different types of vertical relationships
with another firm. It can sell products to that firm (seller
relationship) and it can purchase products from that firm (buyer
relationship). Vertical interdependence arises when the behavior
of a firm in one market is affected by the vertical relationships
it has with one or more of its competitors in that market. In
this section, measures of vertical interdependence will be derived
for these two types of vertical relationships.

1. Seller Relationships

It is assumed that firms A and B are once again direct
competitors in market one and that A also has a vertical seller
relationship with B in market two. More specifically, A sells
Q_2 to B which uses it as an input in its manufacturing operations.
A's vertical interdependence with B from this sales contact results
from the prospect that B might change suppliers. This potential
sales loss is hypothesized to moderate A's behavior toward B
when they interact as direct competitors in market one. If A
is aggressive toward B in that market, B may retaliate by
switching suppliers, thereby reducing A's sales of Q_2.

A's perceived vertical interdependence with B will be proxied
by the elasticity of A's profits with respect to its sales of Q_2 to
B. This will give us a measure of vertical seller interdependence
(VSI) consistent with the "profit senstivity" criterion and a
vertical counterpart to the horizontal measure derived in the

preceding section.

Assuming that A produces in only these two markets, its total profits can be written as

$$(10) \qquad \Pi_A = P_{A1}Q_{A1} - C_{A1} + P_{A2}Q_{A2} - C_{A2}$$

where, P_{A1}, Q_{A1} and C_{A1} are A's price, output level and total production costs in market one, etc.

The impact on A's profits of B switching to another supplier is simply the profit margin which A would have earned on those sales to B. The sensitivity of A's profits to an incremental change in B's purchases can be analyzed by taking the partial derivative of (10) with respect to B's purchases of Q_2 (Q_{B2}^*, where the asterik indicates purchases, not production of Q_2 by firm B).

$$(11) \qquad \frac{\partial \Pi_A}{\partial Q_{B2}^*} = P_{A2} \frac{\partial Q_{A2}}{\partial Q_{B2}^*} - C'_{A2} \frac{\partial Q_{A2}}{\partial Q_{B2}^*} = (P_{A2} - C'_{A2}) \frac{\partial Q_{A2}}{\partial Q_{B2}^*}$$

The elasticity of A's profits with respect to purchases by B can be derived in a similar manner to that used in the horizontal case.

First, both sides of (11) are multiplied by Q_{B2}^*/Π_A which automatically puts the left side of (12) in elasticity form --

$$\eta_{\Pi_A, Q_B^*}$$

$$(12) \qquad \frac{\partial \Pi_A}{\partial Q_{B2}^*} \cdot \frac{Q_{B2}^*}{\Pi_A} = (P_{A2} - C'_{A2}) \frac{\partial Q_{A2}}{\partial Q_{B2}^*} \cdot \frac{Q_{B2}^*}{\Pi_A}$$

Next, the right side is multiplied by a well-chosen one (Q_{A2}/Q_{A2}).

$$\eta_{\Pi_A, Q_B^*} = (P_{A2} - C'_{A2}) \frac{\partial Q_{A2}}{\partial Q_{B2}^*} \cdot \frac{Q_{B2}^*}{\Pi_A} \cdot \frac{Q_{A2}}{Q_{A2}}$$

which, after rearranging terms, is equivalent to

(13) $$\eta_{\Pi_A, Q_B^*} = \frac{(P_{A2} - C'_{A2})Q_{A2}}{\Pi_A} \left(\frac{\partial Q_{A2}}{\partial Q_{B2}^*} \cdot \frac{Q_{B2}^*}{Q_{A2}} \right)$$

The expression in brackets is simply the elasticity of A's sales (in quantity terms) with respect to B's purchases (also in quantity terms). This elasticity can be simplified by noting that since Q_{B2}^* is purchases from A, $\partial Q_{A2}/\partial Q_{B2}^*$ equals one. A's sales will increase (decrease) by one for every additional unit purchased (withdrawn) from A by B. Also, Q_{A2} is simply A's market share of market two (MS_{A2}) times total market output (Q_2), while Q_{B2}^* is B's buyer's share of market two (BS_{B2}) times market output (Q_2).

$$Q_{A2} = MS_{A2} \cdot Q_2$$

$$Q_{B2}^* = BS_{B2} \cdot Q_2$$

Substituting the above relationships into (13) gives us

(14) $$\eta_{\Pi_A, Q_B^*} = \frac{(P_{A2} - C'_{A2})Q_{A2}}{\Pi_A} \left(1 \cdot \frac{BS_{B2}}{MS_{A2}} \cdot \frac{Q_2}{Q_2} \right)$$

which, after cancelling Q_2 and making the same substitutions as in the horizontal case, leaves us with a measure of vertical seller interdependence (VSI) which can be empirically estimated.

$$(15) \qquad VSI_{AB} = \frac{M_{A2}}{M_A} \cdot \frac{BS_{B2}}{MS_{A2}}$$

where M_A is firm margins and M_{A2} is A's margins from its sales of Q_2.

A's vertical seller interdependence with B is therefore a function of the relative contribution of that market to total firm margin and the relative size of B's purchases of Q_2 compared to A's production of Q_2.

As in the horizontal case, the measure can be extended to capture all of the vertical seller relationships that A might have with B by summing over the j markets in which A produces.

$$(16) \qquad VSI_{AB} = \sum_j \frac{M_{Aj}}{M_A} \cdot \frac{BS_{Bj}}{MS_{Aj}}$$

A's vertical interdependence on the seller side with any m competitors in the jth market is simply the sum of (16) over all m competitors.

$$(17) \qquad VSI_{Am} = \sum_m \sum_j \frac{M_{Aj}}{M_A} \cdot \frac{BS_{mj}}{MS_{Aj}}$$

The measure of vertical seller interdependence increases with increases in the relative contribution of that market to total firm margin and the buyer's share of the competitors.

2. Buyer Relationships

It is assumed that A and B meet as direct competitors in one market and that A has a vertical buyer relationship with competitor B. Firm B produces Q_3 which A purchases for use as an input somewhere in its manufacturing operations. A's vertical interdependence with B from this buyer contact results from the potential foreclosure of A from this input source. It is hypothesized that A will moderate its behavior toward B when they meet as direct competitors for fear of being foreclosed from Q_3 by competitor B.

The problem now is how to derive a profit elasticity measure which reflects the sensitivity of A's profits to the possibility of foreclosure by B. This is more difficult than in the horizontal and vertical seller cases since there is no obvious direct link between the competitor's action of foreclosure and A's profitability. To obtain such a link it is necessary to make an assumption about every one of the firm's production functions which uses this particular input. The degree of vertical interdependence will vary drastically with the assumption made about the marginal rate of technical substitution of this input with other inputs. At the extremes, foreclosure from this input could completely stop production or, not affect it at all.

Without specific knowledge of the firm's production function

for each industry in which it operates, it is not possible to
determine the direct effect of an input foreclosure by B on
A's profits. The alternative approach adopted in this thesis
was to construct an "intuitive" measure of vertical buyer interdependence (VBI). There are two issues which must be addressed
in this area. First, what determines firm A's recognition of the
relative importance of a specific input to its production effort.
And secondly, how can we proxy the foreclosure threat posed by an
input supplier.

With respect to the first issue, it was assumed that a
firm's recognition of the importance of an input was a function
of the expenditures on that input as a percent of total production
costs. As the relative expenditures on this input increase, so
should the perceived vertical interdependence with firms which
supply that input. The second issue was solved by using the
supplier's market share in the input industry to proxy the foreclosure threat. The threat of foreclosure will be greater, the
smaller is the alternate supply, which is inversely related to
the supplier's market share. The threat of foreclosure is therefore
posited to be a positive function of the supplier's market share.

For the original example of A and B, A's perceived vertical
buyer interdependence with B will be defined as

$$(18) \qquad VBI_{AB} = \frac{C_{A3}}{C_A} \cdot MS_{B3}$$

where C_{A3} is firm A's total expenditures on Q_3, C_A is firm A's total costs across all of its operations, and MS_{B3} is firm B's market share in market three. The cost data will be derived from the firm's estimated sales and the industry cost structures given in the Department of Commerce's input-ouptut tables (See Chapter V). As defined here, A's perceived vertical interdependence with B will increase with increases in the relative importance of that input to A (as measured in dollar terms) and with increases in the market position of competitor B.

When firm A purchases more than one input from B, (18) will be summed over all of the products which B produces

$$(19) \qquad VBI_{AB} = \sum_j \frac{C_{Aj}}{C_A} \cdot MS_{Bj}$$

where j is the industries in which B produces, C_{Aj} is A's purchases of the jth product from B and MS_{Bj} is firm B's market share of the jth market. If A does not purchase any product from B in the jth market, C_{Aj} will equal zero and that industry will not affect A's vertical interdependence with B.

To capture firm A's vertical buyer interdependence with all of its m competitors in a given industry, (19) is summed over those m firms.

$$(20) \qquad VBI_{Am} = \sum_m \sum_j \frac{C_{Aj}}{C_A} \cdot MS_{mj}$$

Before concluding this section, one important difference in the horizontal and vertical measures should be emphasized. In the horizontal case the perceived interdependence between firms depends on the market under analysis since the measure will not be summed over that market. Only external contacts are measured in accordance with the assumptions of the mutual forbearance hypothesis. This is not the case with the vertical measures. These measures are independent of the market of analysis since vertical relationships are always external to the markets where horizontal contacts occur. A's vertical interdependence with B will be the same irrespective of the market in which they meet as direct competitors.

C. Aggregation Issues

Aggregation issues arise at both the firm and market level of analysis. At the firm level, the central issue is whether the horizontal and vertical measures of interdependence can be aggregated into a single measure of total firm interdependence. And, if so, is such a measure meaningful in terms of testing the mutual forbearance hypothesis. At the market level, the aggregation issue deals with the transformation of the individual firm measures into a single market measure which can be used in cross-section analyses of the determinants of industry price-cost margins.

With respect to the first issue, it appears to be one of trying to add apples and oranges. Each measure captures a unique type of interfirm relationship and was derived under different

assumptions and using different proxy variables. The usefulness
of these measures could easily be lost through aggregation. By
keeping the measures separate, however, it is possible to test
the individual effect of these horizontal and vertical relationships. This seems highly desirable from a policy perspective.
Also, the joint influence of these measures can always be captured
through interaction terms. In short, there does not appear to
be any advantage to aggregating the three measures into a single
measure. Separate measures of interdependence will therefore be
constructed for each firm.

The next step is to determine the proper scheme for aggregating
the firm measures of horizontal and vertical interdependence into
industry measures which can be used in cross-section analyses of
market performance. As noted in the first section of this chapter,
multi-market contacts are hypothesized to increase firm interdependence, thereby facilitating overt and/or covert collusion.
This collusion will enable an industry's firms to restrict output
and approach the joint-profit maximizing output levels. The effect
on industry price will depend on the relative magnitude of the
firm's output changes and the price elasticity of market demand.

Assume that, once again, firms A and B compete in market
one. Market output is the sum of the individual firms' outputs

(21) $$Q_1 = Q_{A1} + Q_{B1} + \sum_m Q_{m1}$$

where m is the number of other firms in market one. Any incremental change in market output is the sum of individual firm changes in their output level.

(22) $\qquad \Delta Q_1 = \Delta Q_{A1} + \Delta Q_{B1} + \sum_m \Delta Q_{m1}$

Dividing (22) by Q_1 and a well-chosen one enables us to express the percentage change in market one's output as a weighted average of the percentage changes in the firm's outputs

(23) $\qquad \dfrac{\Delta Q_1}{Q_1} = MS_{A1} \cdot \dfrac{\Delta Q_{A1}}{Q_{A1}} + MS_{B2} \cdot \dfrac{\Delta Q_{B1}}{Q_{B1}} + \sum_m MS_{m1} \cdot \dfrac{\Delta Q_{m1}}{Q_{m1}}$

where the weights are the firms' market shares (MS_{m1}).

The percentage change in a firm's output is hypothesized to be a function of the firm's interdependence with its competitors. The percentage change in the industry's output will, therefore, be a function of the weighted averages of the firm measures of vertical and horizontal interdependence. The industry measures of horizontal (HI) and vertical buyer (VBI) and seller (VSI) interdependence will be equal to

(24) $\qquad HI = \sum_n MS_{nk} \cdot HI_{nk}$

(25) $\qquad VBI = \sum_n MS_{nk} \cdot VBI_{nk}$

(26) $\qquad VSI = \sum_n MS_{nk} \cdot VSI_{nk}$

where n is the number of firms in the kth industry, MS_{nk} is the market share of the nth firm, and HI_{nk}, VBI_{nk} and VSI_{nk} are the nth firm's perceived interdependence arising from external contacts with its n-1 competitors.

FOOTNOTES

[1]If firms A and B interact in two markets, A's profits will equal the sum of the profits from these two markets.

(1) $\qquad \Pi_A = \Pi_{A1} + \Pi_{A2}$

The differential of A's profits with respect to B's output will then be

(2) $\qquad d\Pi_A = \dfrac{\partial \Pi_{A1}}{\partial Q_{B1}} \cdot dQ_{B1} + \dfrac{\partial \Pi_{A2}}{\partial Q_{B2}} \cdot dQ_{B2}$

Dividing by Π_A and multiplying by well-chosen ones gives us

(3) $\qquad \dfrac{d\Pi_A}{\Pi_A} = \dfrac{\Pi_{A1}}{\Pi_{A1}} \cdot \dfrac{Q_{B1}}{Q_{B1}} \left(\dfrac{\partial \Pi_{A1}}{\partial Q_{B1}} \right) \dfrac{dQ_{B1}}{\Pi_A}$

$\qquad + \dfrac{\Pi_{A2}}{\Pi_{A2}} \cdot \dfrac{Q_{B2}}{Q_{B2}} \left(\dfrac{\partial \Pi_{A2}}{\partial Q_{B2}} \right) \dfrac{dQ_{B2}}{\Pi_A}$

which, after rearranging terms, equals

(4) $\qquad \dfrac{d\Pi_A}{\Pi_A} = \dfrac{\Pi_{A1}}{\Pi_A} \left(\dfrac{\partial \Pi_{A1}}{\partial Q_{B1}} \cdot \dfrac{Q_{B1}}{\Pi_{A1}} \right) \dfrac{dQ_{B1}}{Q_{B1}}$

$\qquad + \dfrac{\Pi_{A2}}{\Pi_A} \left(\dfrac{\partial \Pi_{A2}}{\partial Q_{B2}} \cdot \dfrac{Q_{B2}}{\Pi_{A2}} \right) \dfrac{dQ_{B2}}{Q_{B2}}$

where the figures in parentheses are the elasticities of A's
profits in each market with respect to B's outputs in those
markets ($\eta_{\Pi_{A1}, Q_{B1}}$ and $\eta_{\Pi_{A2}, Q_{B2}}$). (4) can thus be written

$$(5) \qquad \frac{d\Pi_A}{\Pi_A} = \frac{\Pi_{A1}}{\Pi_A} \cdot \eta_{\Pi_{A1}, Q_{B1}} \cdot \frac{dQ_{B1}}{Q_{B1}}$$

$$+ \frac{\Pi_{A2}}{\Pi_A} \cdot \eta_{\Pi_{A2}, Q_{B2}} \cdot \frac{dQ_{B2}}{Q_{B2}}$$

Since we want the total elasticity of A's profits with respect
to B's output, we define the percentage change in B's output to
be the same in both markets:

$$\frac{dQ_{B1}}{Q_{B1}} = \frac{dQ_{B2}}{Q_{B2}} .$$

This enables us to divide (5) by the percentage change in B's
output and end up with the following relationship.

$$(5) \qquad \eta_{\Pi_A, Q_B} = \frac{\Pi_{A1}}{\Pi_A} \cdot \eta_{\Pi_{A1}, Q_{B1}} + \frac{\Pi_{A2}}{\Pi_A} \cdot \eta_{\Pi_{A2}, Q_{B2}}$$

Thus, the total elasticity of A's profits with respect to B's
output is simply a weighted average of the individual market
elasticities, where the weights are the market's relative
contribution to total profits.

APPENDIX A

A Simple Model of Firm Interdependence

The relationship between firm interdependence and industry profitability can be conveniently analyzed with duopoly models. To simplify matters only horizontal relationships will be examined. The approach adopted, however, can easily be extended to analyze vertical relationships.

A horizontal relationship exists between two firms when they meet as competitors in a given industry. Horizontal inter-industry interdependence (HII) arises when those firms meet as competitors in two or more industries and those contacts in other industries affect their behavior toward each other in a single industry. The firm perceives the fortunes of the industries to be interrelated. To illustrate the concept of HII and examine its effect on firm behavior, we will use a simple model of two firms (A and B) who meet as duopolists in two separate industries.

Firms A and B are assumed to produce homogeneous products in industries 1 and 2. The inverse demand functions for the two industries relate price to the quantity sold:

(1) $P_1 = P_1(Q_{A1} + Q_{B1})$

(2) $P_2 = P_2(Q_{A2} + Q_{B2})$

where Q_{A1} is firm A's output in industry 1, etc., and all of the first partial derivatives of industry price with respect to firm output are negative.

The crucial assumption of the mutual forbearance hypothesis is captured in the following equations:

(3) $\qquad Q_{B1} = G_1(Q_{A1}, Q_{A2})$

(4) $\qquad Q_{B2} = G_2(Q_{A1}, Q_{A2})$

where G_1 and G_2 are functions relating firm B's output in a single industry to A's output level in both industries. More specifically, these functions are conjectures by firm A of firm B's reaction functions. These conjectural variation functions are at the heart of the mutual forbearance hypothesis for they make output decisions in all industries interdependent. If firm A changes its output level in one industry, this will affect B's output level, as well as the industry price and A's profits, in both industries.

The next step is to examine the effect of firm A's perceived interdependence with firm B on A's output decisions in industries 1 and 2. Assume that firm A's total costs are given by

(5) $\qquad C_{A1} = C_1(Q_{A1})$

(6) $\qquad C_{A2} = C_2(Q_{A2})$

Then, substituting (3) and (4) into (1) and (2), firm A's total profits can be written as

(7) $\qquad \pi_A = P_1[Q_{A1} + G_1(Q_{A1}, Q_{A2})]Q_{A1} - C_1(Q_{A1}) +$

$\qquad\qquad P_2[Q_{A2} + G_2(Q_{A1}, Q_{A2})]Q_{A2} - C_2(Q_{A2})$

Setting the first partial derivatives of (7) with respect to Q_{A1} and Q_{A2} equal to zero, we obtain the first-order conditions necessary for A to maximize profits given its perceived interdependence with B.

$$(8) \quad \frac{\partial \pi_A}{\partial Q_{A1}} = P_1 + Q_{A1}P_1'[1 + \frac{\partial G_1}{\partial Q_{A1}}] - C_{A1}' + Q_{A2}P_2' \frac{\partial G_2}{\partial Q_{A1}} = 0$$

$$(9) \quad \frac{\partial \pi_A}{\partial Q_{A2}} = Q_{A1}P_1' \frac{\partial G_1}{\partial Q_{A2}} + P_2 + Q_{A2}P_2'[1 + \frac{\partial G_2}{\partial Q_{A2}}] - C_{A2}' = 0$$

As expected, the first-order conditions indicate that profit maximization requires marginal revenue to equal marginal cost in each industry. The interesting thing to note about (8) and (9) is that marginal revenue in one industry is dependent upon the output level in the other industry. This result follows from (3) and (4) which introduced the conjectural variation terms $\partial G_2 / \partial Q_{A1}$ and $\partial G_1 / \partial Q_{A2}$. If these terms equal zero, contacts in other industries will have no effect on output decisions within a particular industry. In such a case, firm A's output level in one industry will only be influenced by firm B's presence in that industry as captured by $\partial G_1 / \partial Q_{A1}$ or $\partial G_2 / \partial Q_{A2}$.

The effect of horizontal interdependence on firm A's profit maximization calculus can be seen more clearly by writing (8) and (9) in the following form:

$$(10) \quad Q_{A1} = \frac{C'_{A1} - P_1 - Q_{A2}P'_2 \dfrac{\partial G_2}{\partial Q_{A1}}}{P'_1 \left[1 + \dfrac{\partial G_1}{\partial Q_{A1}}\right]}$$

$$(11) \quad Q_{A2} = \frac{C'_{A2} - P_2 - Q_{A1}P'_1 \dfrac{\partial G_1}{\partial Q_{A2}}}{P'_2 \left[1 + \dfrac{\partial G_2}{\partial Q_{A2}}\right]}$$

Several implications of (10) and (11) should be emphasized. First, if all four conjectural variation terms equal zero, firm A will produce the output levels predicted by the Cournot duopoly model:

$$Q_{A1} = \frac{C'_{A1} - P_1}{P'_1} \qquad\qquad Q_{A2} = \frac{C'_{A2} - P_2}{P'_2}$$

This is not a surprising result since setting the conjectural variation terms equal to zero fulfills the Cournot assumption that firms behave as if their rival's output level is constant. Cournot firms do not recognize their interdependence from competing in the same industry, much less from competing across several industries. Secondly, as noted before, there are two different "types" of conjectural variation terms. One "type", $\partial G_1/\partial Q_{A1}$, captures the perceived interdependence from being a competitor in industry 1 with firm B, while the other "type", $\partial G_2/\partial Q_{A1}$, incorporates the perceived interdependence arising from A's interactions with B outside industry 1. The same considerations apply in industry 2.

These terms indicate that firm A's total perceived interdependence with firm B is a function of horizontal inter-industry and intra-industry interdependence. Thirdly, the effect of horizontal interdependence on firm A's output levels depends on the sign and magnitude of the conjectural variation terms. The mutual forbearance hypothesis argues that firms will react aggressively to output expansion by their competitors, which would indicate positive first partials. In such a case, interdependence due to intra-industry and inter-industry contacts operates to reduce A's output levels. To illustrate this point, look at (10). Interdependence due to outside contacts (industry 2) reduces Q_{A1} by decreasing the numerator, while interdependence from competing directly in market 1 reduces Q_{A1} by increasing the denominator. Thus, firm A's perceived interdependence with firm B in markets 1 and 2 operates to decrease its output level in both markets.

CHAPTER III

The Sample

The measures of firm interdependence developed in Chapter II
are functions of firm market shares. A firm's sales to and/or
purchases from an industry, as well as its competitors' market
power in that industry, are all derived from market share data.
Unfortunately such data is not available in sufficient detail for
a large sample of leading American firms. It was thus necessary
to estimate a firm's market share in all of the industries in
which it operated. The approach adopted in this thesis was to
estimate a firm's market share with its estimated share of industry
employment. This chapter describes the methodology used to obtain
such data and provides some descriptive statistics for the sample
firms.

There are two sources which identify the manufacturing industries of leading American firms: Dun's "Market Identifiers" and
Fortune's _Plant_ _and_ _Product_ _Directory_. Dun and Bradstreet provide
more current data (they began their service in 1972), but this
avenue was not pursued due to the prohibitive expense. Attempts
to obtain this information from private individuals and government
agencies which had access to it were unsuccessful. It was then
decided to use Fortune's data to estimate firm market shares.

Fortune's _Directory_ first appeared in 1960 and covered the
industrial operations of the 500 leading American industrial corporations (based on annual sales). This coverage was extended to

the top 1,000 industrials in the two subsequent editions (1963–1964 and 1966). Publication of the Directory ceased with the 1966 edition.

The initial sample consisted of 465 firms and was generously provided by Leonard Weiss. All of these firms were among the top 1,000 domestic industrials (173 were in the top 200) based on 1963 annual sales. The procedure employed by Weiss to estimate firm employment at the industry level is described below. The final sample was restricted to only top 200 firms (twenty-two were added to the initial 173[1]) for two reasons. First, most of the concern over firm conglomeration focused on the acquisition activities of these firms [F.T.C. (1969), Mueller (1971)]. These firms are the most diversified and provide fertile terrain for the hypothesized anticompetitive practices associated with diversified firms. Secondly, it soon became apparent that it would be impossible to use the initial sample of 465 firms given the author's time and financial constraints.

The manufacturing activities of the sample firms were obtained from the 1963–1964 Fortune Directory, which lists every four-digit manufacturing industry (S.I.C.) in which a firm was active during this period. Based on survey responses, Fortune assigned a firm's plants to one or more S.I.C.'s depending on the composition of their output. For example, International Business Machines (IBM) operated fourteen plants in six four-digit industries during this period. Nine of these plants produced only one five-digit

product, while four plants produced two and the remaining plant

produced four. At the four-digit level, only two plants pro-

duced products classified in more than one four-digit industry

(two in one and three in the other).

In addition to classifying a firm's plants by industry, the

Directory provides a rough estimate of each plant's total employ-

ment. When information permitted, each plant was assigned to

one of the following employment categories:

Category	Employment Range
A	0-99
B	100-499
C	500-999
D	1000-4999
E	5000 and over

There are two problems which must be surmounted, however, before

this data can be used to estimate market shares. First, how can

these employment ranges be turned into more exact estimates of

plant employment? Secondly, assuming that better estimates can

be obtained, how should these estimates of plant employment be

allocated among a plant's products?

The following procedure was adopted to surmount the first

problem -- the estimation of plant employment. If a plant's

employment category was A, B or C, it was automatically assigned

the mid-point value of that category (50, 300 and 750 respectively).

For example, the employment of IBM's Greencastle, Indiana plant

(category C) was listed as 750, while its Dayton, New Jersey
plant (category B) was given 300. Since the absolute estimation
error increases substantially with increases in plant size, an
effort was made to obtain more detailed employment estimates for
D and E size plants. The Fortune data was supplemented with
information from state and city directories and letters written
to plant managers and city chambers of commerce. If these actions
did not produce any additional information, two alternatives
were available. Use the average employment of similar sized plants
based on census data, or utilize the information inherent in
the firm's total employment figure. In the latter case, a large
plant's employment could be estimated by subtracting the employment of the "known" plants from the firm's total employment
figure. In such cases, the firm's total employment figure was
obtained from the 1964 edition of Moody's Industrials.

If a plant's employment classification was "not available",
several different avenues were explored in an effort to determine
the plant's employment. If a firm had several other plants in the
same industry whose employment was known, an average of those plants
could be used for the unknown plant. This situation rarely
arose. In some cases the average size of a four-digit plant could
be used, but these generally tended to be so small as almost to
be insignificant. If the above approaches were not fruitful, the
plant was dropped from the analysis. This situation was rare
except for a few firms which had to be dropped from the sample --
e.g., National Dairy Products, Standard Brands and Westinghouse.

Once a plant's employment was estimated, it had to be allocated among the different products produced by that plant. In general, plant employment was distributed evenly among the five-digit products it produced -- i.e., it was assumed that all products were of equal importance unless there was information to the contrary. Four-digit industry employment was obtained by summing the employment of five-digit products with the identical first four digits of their product code. Following this rule, the employment of IBM's Burlington, Vermont plant (employment category C) was divided equally between the two five-digit products produced at that plant: 35712 (computing and accounting machines) and 36133 (low voltage panelboards). Since these products were in different industries, 3571 and 3613, each industry was credited with an additional 375 employees. If both products had been in the same industry, the entire employment of 750 would have been allocated to that industry. By proceeding in this manner for all of a firm's plants, it was possible to estimate a firm's employment in every manufacturing industry in which it was active in 1963.

I checked the accuracy of these employment estimates at both the firm and industry level. At the firm level, a firm's estimated total employment was compared to its actual total employment for 1963. This comparison was hindered by deficiencies in the Moody's total employment figures. First of all, it was not always clear whether the figure stated was for domestic or worldwide employment. This was a problem for the sample under consideration since most of them operated foreign plants. Secondly, the employment figure listed in Moody's depended on the consolidation practice used by each firm -- i.e., consolidating employment from all subsidiaries where a firm had a controlling interest (> 50%) or only those which were wholly owned by the parent corporation. Thirdly, the Moody's figure was for total firm employment while that estimated from plant data was only for manufacturing. Actual employment should exceed estimated employment if a firm was substantially engaged in non-manufacturing activities such as transportation and distribution. These points are mentioned to stress the fact that determining a firm's total employment, much less allocating it to specific industries, is less than an exact science and that there are many reasons why the two figures will, and should, differ.

Given the above qualifications, estimated employment was compared to actual employment for consistency. If estimated employment seemed reasonable in light of the limitations discussed above, it was accepted. This generally meant that the estimated figure did not exceed the actual figure and that all of a firm's major plants (as listed in Moody's) were accounted for in the Fortune data. Estimated employment exceeded actual employment for eleven firms. Due to the questionable reliability of the actual employment figures, the estimated employment figure was accepted without modification if it exceeded the actual figure by ten percent or less. If the difference was greater than this, a "compromise" figure ten percent larger than actual employment was used and plant employment figures were reduced proportionately.

After the employment estimates had been examined at the firm level, they were examined for consistency at the industry level. The main issue here was whether the allocation of the firms' employment across industries was consistent with industry concentration data. The percentage of an industry's labor force attributed to the sample firms was compared to the appropriate concentration ratio for industry value of shipments. Even though the concentration ratios for value of shipments and employment tend to be very similar, the value of shipments ratios were used instead since the firms' labor shares are proxies for their market shares. If the sample firms' percentage was greater (less) than the appropriate concentration percentage and the sample firms were the leading firms in that industry, their sum of shares, and hence their individual shares as well, were adjusted downward (upward) to equal that percentage. If the sample firms were not the leading firms in the industry, their sum was compared to a modified concentration ratio (typically comparing their share to some portion of the concentration ratio). If their shares were consistent with the concentration data -- less than or equal to the extrapolated values -- they were not changed.

The sample firms' market shares were inconsistent with concentration data in 31 of the 417 manufacturing industries. These differences generally arose for two reasons. First, the mid-point values were bad approximations to the actual employment of A, B and C category plants. This was especially a problem in industries

dominated by these plants. In such cases, the mid-point values
were replaced by averages based on census establishment data. For
example, in the ice cream and frozen desserts industry (2024), A
and B plants were given total employments of 20 and 170 instead of
the mid-point values 50 and 300. The second problem concerned the
allocation of plant employment across industries for large plants --
those in the D and E size categories. If a plant's employment was
allocated equally among its products, market shares were distorted
if one of the products was only a "minor" product in relation to
the others. This "minor" product would then be credited with too
much employment and its market share would be inconsistent with concentration data. The solution adopted was to reduce this product's
employment to the maximum value consistent with census establishment
data. For the Whirlpool Corporation this meant reducing their
employment share in the commercial laundry equipment industry (3582)
from .476 to .234, while augmenting their original share in the
household laundry industry (3633) from .170 to .236.[2]

Using the procedure outlined in this chapter, it was possible
to construct market share data for 195 of the top 200 industrial
corporations in 1963. As noted earlier, Westinghouse Electric,
National Dairy Products and Standard Brands were excluded from the
sample for lack of plant employment estimates. The two remaining
firms, Ogden and International Packers, were inexplicably omitted
from the Fortune Directory and had to be dropped.

The final sample of 195 firms is listed in the Appendix to this
chapter. An average sample firm operated in 13.6 manufacturing

industries in 1963. The distribution of sample firms by number of manufacturing industries is given in the table below. At the extremes, four firms (Gulf Oil, Mack Trucks, Richfield Oil and Sunray DX Oil) were active in only one industry, while the most diversified firm, General Electric, was active in 76 industries. It should be noted that one fourth of these firms, the leading firms in the economy, were active in five or less industries.

Numbers of industries by themselves, however, do not indicate the extent to which a firm's productive resources are distributed among those industries. Berry's index of firm diversification is designed to surmount this problem [Berry (1971)]. This measure is defined as:

$$BI = 1 - \sum_{j} p_j^2$$

where p_j is the percentage of a firm's sales originating in the jth industry. This index equals zero if a firm produces in only one industry and approaches one if a firm's sales are spread evenly among many industries. Also, when a firm's sales are divided equally among n industries the index will equal $1 - \frac{1}{n}$.

The Berry index ranges from .0000 (for the four firms in a single industry) to .9575 (General Electric) for the sample firms. The mean value is .5712 which is equivalent to a firm having equal sales in 2.3 industries. These findings are consistent with Berry's previous work on firm diversification [Berry (1971)]. A surprising result is the non-significant correlation between estimated firm

TABLE IV

Distribution of Firms by Number of

Manufacturing Industries

	Number of Firms	Percentage of Firms
1-5	49	25.1
6-10	42	21.5
11-15	39	20.0
16-20	27	13.8
21-25	13	6.7
26-30	11	5.6
31-35	6	3.1
36-40	3	1.5
41+	5	2.6
Total	195	100.0

sales and Berry's diversification index. The simple correlation
between the two is -.0796 while the correlation between estimated
sales and number of industries is .4381. These correlations
suggest that even though large firms (in terms of annual sales)
are more diversified, that diversification may be characterized
more by breadth than depth.

At the industry level, the sample firms were active in
353 of the 417 manufacturing industries. In an average one of
these industries there were 7.5 sample firms and they had a combined
market share of .2764. The range of the sample firms' combined
market share is illustrated in Table V. This data indicates
that sample firms controlled more than fifty percent of sales in
60 of the 417 manufacturing S.I.C.'s in 1963.

TABLE V

Distribution of Industries by Sample Firms'

Combined Market Share

	Number of Industries	Percentage of Industries
.0000-.1000	179	42.9
.1001-.2000	54	12.9
.2001-.3000	46	11.0
.3001-.4000	46	11.0
.4001-.5000	32	7.7
.5001-.6000	15	3.6
.6001-.7000	16	3.8
.7001-.8000	12	2.9
.8001-.9000	8	1.9
.9001+	9	2.2
Total	417	100.0

FOOTNOTES

[1]My employment estimates for these twenty-two firms were based on the 1963-1964 Fortune Directory and were supplemented with information from the 1964 Moody's Industrials and the 1963 Census of Manufactures. State and city directories were not used nor were letters written to plant managers concerning these firms.

[2]The sensitivity of the market share data with respect to my adjustments was examined for a randomly selected sample of nineteen firms. These firms were active in a total of 222 industries and twenty-nine (13.1%) of these market shares were affected by one or both of the checks I used. The mean value of the final market share estimates was .0302 compared to .0351 for the "uncorrected" estimates, while the simple correlation between the two was .8868. Since these adjustments were designed to reduce measurement error in the original data, it is not clear what bias, if any, they impart to the results obtained in this thesis.

APPENDIX B

Sample Firms

Firm	Fortune Rank	Number of Manufacturing Industries	Berry Index
Air Reduction	180	16	.8433
Allied Chemical	55	18	.8710
Allis-Chalmers	104	16	.8935
Aluminum Company of America	51	16	.6841
American Can	41	17	.7125
American Cynamid	71	19	.8821
American Home Products	108	13	.8022
American Machine & Foundry	157	28	.9273
American Metal Climax	73	17	.8691
American Motors	44	4	.0909
American Radiator & Standard Sanitary	109	20	.8747
American Smelting & Refining	103	11	.7517
American Sugar	130	4	.1683
American Tobacco	77	3	.2373
Anaconda	72	14	.7479
Anheuser-Busch	163	9	.7025
Armco Steel	57	10	.4397
Armour	23	22	.6222
Armstrong Cork	165	13	.8639
Ashland Oil & Refining	153	2	.0068
Atlantic Refining	85	4	.2071
Avco	111	13	.8612
Babcock & Wilcox	148	12	.8551
Beatrice Foods	99	12	.7746
Bendix	63	44	.8780
Bethlehem Steel	17	8	.3364
Boeing	25	2	.0829
Borden	45	35	.7509
Borg-Warner	76	43	.8671
Brown Shoe	176	15	.6606
Brunswick	177	12	.7074
Budd	174	11	.6224
Burlington Industries	48	21	.8730
Burroughs	145	14	.5067

Firm	Fortune Rank	Number of Manufacturing Industries	Berry Index
California Packing	146	7	.2888
Campbell Soup	82	6	.6940
Carnation	131	9	.7647
Carrier	186	8	.4114
Caterpillar Tractor	54	2	.4710
Celanese	159	8	.6904
Central Soya	164	2	.3629
Champion Papers	154	11	.8299
Chrysler	7	18	.1948
Cities Service	37	5	.0774
Coca-Cola	83	5	.4293
Colgate-Palmolive	70	3	.4874
Combustion Engineering	192	5	.6103
Consolidation Coal	197	8	.6523
Container Corporation of American	161	9	.7422
Continental Baking	121	6	.3625
Continental Can	40	17	.7039
Continental Oil	42	6	.0343
Corn Products	58	11	.7469
Corning Glass Works	195	6	.2669
Crane	167	18	.8128
Crown Zellerbach	88	11	.8378
Cudahy Packing	171	8	.5099
Dana	178	7	.3434
Deere	81	7	.5611
Douglas Aircraft	75	3	.5416
Dow Chemical	52	30	.8969
Dupont (E.I.) de Nemours	11	39	.8410
Eastman Kodak	47	8	.4229
Eaton Manufacturing	117	21	.4126
FMC	87	34	.8833
Firestone Tire & Rubber	32	24	.6352
Ford Motor	3	33	.3224
Foremost Dairies	139	8	.6939
General American Transportation	196	19	.7750
General Dynamics	30	28	.8680
General Electric	4	76	.9575
General Foods	36	28	.8759
General Mills	110	22	.6529
General Motors	1	58	.3785

Firm	Fortune Rank	Number of Manufacturing Industries	Berry Index
General Telephone & Electronics	29	29	.9054
General Tire	49	23	.8330
Genesco	141	19	.7048
Georgia-Pacific	127	10	.7741
Gillette	187	4	.2999
Goodrich (B.F.)	62	24	.8030
Goodyear Tire & Rubber	26	11	.7231
Grace (W.R.)	92	32	.8361
Grumman Aircraft Engineering	123	5	.4740
Gulf Oil	9	1	.0000
Heinz (H.J.)	126	5	.7351
Hercules Powder	120	16	.8419
Hormel (Geo. A.)	143	2	.4232
Hunt Foods & Industries	142	22	.8696
Hygrade Food Products	132	7	.5398
Inland Steel	64	8	.1763
International Business Machines	18	6	.3172
International Harvester	19	12	.5376
International Milling	179	2	.3274
International Paper	43	16	.7793
International Shoe	188	6	.4758
International Telephone & Telegraph	31	13	.7228
Johns-Manville	134	18	.8151
Johnson & Johnson	156	14	.8524
Jones & Laughlin Steel	61	9	.3604
Kaiser Aluminum & Chemical	129	14	.7361
Kaiser Industries	160	5	.0700
Kellogg	173	3	.2917
Kennecott Copper	112	4	.6864
Kimberly-Clark	105	15	.7354
Koppers	189	12	.7810
Lever Brothers	133	5	.4745
Liggett & Myers Tobacco	194	2	.0918
Ling-Temco-Vought	168	18	.8300
Litton Industries	102	31	.8955
Lockheed Aircraft	20	14	.5211
Lorillard (P.)	184	3	.1865

Firm	Fortune Rank	Number of Manufacturing Industries	Berry Index
Mack Trucks	181	1	.0000
Marathon Oil	125	2	.0079
Martin Marietta	53	25	.8742
McDonnell Aircraft	101	7	.6220
McGraw-Edison	152	27	.8868
Mead	124	11	.8378
Minneapolis-Honeywell Regulator	80	13	.8719
Minnesota Mining & Manufacturing	69	26	.9170
Monsanto	39	18	.8691
Morrell (John)	89	3	.3087
Motorola	147	13	.7346
National Biscuit	97	16	.5810
National Cash Register	94	5	.5328
National Distillers & Chemical	122	26	.8780
National Lead	86	20	.8735
National Steel	59	5	.0508
North American Aviation	21	10	.7200
Northrop	162	16	.7920
Olin Mathieson Chemical	67	39	.9418
Owens-Illinois Glass	79	11	.7562
Pfizer (Chas.)	135	15	.7731
Phelps Dodge	169	7	.4996
Philip Morris	144	17	.4302
Phillips Petroleum	34	9	.3016
Pillsbury	137	7	.6011
Pittsburgh Plate Glass	68	21	.8101
Procter & Gamble	28	11	.6893
Pullman	128	4	.5324
Pure Oil	91	2	.0093
Quaker Oats	150	11	.7664
Radio Corporation of America	24	19	.8405
Ralston Purina	65	7	.6353
Raytheon	115	11	.7184
Republic Aviation	155	10	.4970
Republic Steel	46	18	.1906
Rexall Drug & Chemical	200	24	.8738
Reynolds Metals	100	21	.7548

Firm	Fortune Rank	Number of Manufacturing Industries	Berry Index
Reynolds (R.J.) Tobacco	56	3	.0910
Richfield Oil	183	1	.0000
Rockwell-Standard	170	13	.5004
Rohm & Haas	198	6	.6682
St. Regis Paper	93	29	.8896
Scott Paper	151	8	.7010
Seagram (Joseph E.) & Sons	175	5	.0598
Shell Oil	15	10	.3169
Sherwin-Williams	191	14	.7685
Signal Oil & Gas	149	2	.0280
Sinclair Oil	38	6	.0781
Singer	66	18	.8810
Smith (A.O.)	199	24	.5422
Socony Mobil Oil	5	5	.1005
Sperry Rand	35	34	.8191
Standard Oil of California	14	9	.1036
Standard Oil (Ind.)	13	5	.1609
Standard Oil (N.J.)	2	6	.0395
Standard Oil (Ohio)	114	3	.2298
Stevens (J.P.)	90	4	.6641
Studebaker	138	14	.8001
Sun Oil	60	2	.0796
Sunray DX Oil	118	1	.0000
Swift	12	20	.4943
Texaco	8	2	.0062
Textron	95	47	.9444
Thompson Ramo Wooldridge	119	28	.8574
Tidewater Oil	78	3	.0312
Time Inc.	158	11	.5394
Timken Roller Bearing	190	3	.4714
Union Carbide	27	30	.8832
Union Oil of California	113	2	.0331
United Aircraft	33	10	.4776
United Merchants & Manufacturers	116	4	.5037
U.S. Gypsum	182	11	.6558
U.S. Plywood	166	11	.5527
U.S. Rubber	50	17	.7184
U.S. Steel	6	37	.4786

Firm	Fortune Rank	Number of Manufacturing Industries	Berry Index
Warner-Lambert Pharmaceutical	185	11	.8120
West Virginia Pulp & Paper	193	10	.8194
Western Electric	10	7	.6895
Weyerhaeuser	96	14	.8728
Whirlpool	106	7	.7279
White Motor	98	8	.3811
Wilson	74	12	.3104
Youngstown Sheet & Tube	84	9	.5172
Zenith Radio	172	10	.6662

CHAPTER IV

Horizontal Interdependence and Industry Price-Cost Margins

Chapter II provides measures of firm interdependence, both horizontal and vertical, which are consistent with the mutual forbearance hypothesis. In this chapter, the measures of industry horizontal interdependence are estimated for the 195 sample firms described in Chapter III. These measures are then introduced as explanatory variables in a cross-section analysis of industry price-cost margins in 1963.

I. The Model

The industrial organization literature contains many empirical tests of hypothesized relationships between elements of industry structure and performance [Weiss (1971)]. Most of these studies used ordinary least squares regressions to estimate single-equation relationships. This approach is incorrect if the relationship being estimated is part of a simultaneous equations system. This thesis will examine the relationship between firm interdependence and industry price-cost margins using a three-equation simultaneous equations system. The three equations of the system are specified below with y's denoting endogenous variables and x's exogenous variables.

(1)
$$y_1 = \alpha_1 + \gamma_{12}y_2 + \gamma_{13}y_3 + \beta_{11}x_1 + \beta_{12}x_2 + \beta_{13}x_3 + \beta_{14}x_4 + \beta_{15}x_5$$

(2) $$y_2 = \alpha_2 + \gamma_{21}y_1 + \gamma_{23}y_3 + \gamma_{24}y_3^2 + \beta_{23}x_3 + \beta_{25}x_5 + \beta_{26}x_6 + \beta_{27}x_7$$

(3) $$y_3 = \alpha_3 + \gamma_{32}y_2 + \beta_{32}x_2 + \beta_{35}x_5$$

where:

y_1 = industry price-cost margin (M)

y_2 = industry advertising-sales ratio (AD)

y_3 = industry four-firm concentration ratio (CR)

x_1 = industry capital-output ratio (KO)

x_2 = output of mid-point plant as a percent of industry output (MES)

x_3 = rate of growth of industry value of shipments (GR)

x_4 = Collins and Preston index of geographic dispersion of industry industrial activity (GD)

x_5 = industry horizontal interdependence (IHI)

x_6 = ratio of consumer demand to total industry demand (CD)

x_7 = product durability dummy variable (DUR)

The theoretical relationships underlying the equations' structural form have been amply discussed in the literature, [Collins and Preston (1969), Weiss (1971)], so only a brief discussion of each equation will be given below.

A. Industry Price-Cost Margin

The dependent variable, industry price-cost margin, is defined as value of shipments minus direct costs as a percent of value of shipments. It approximates the Lerner index of monopoly power -- price minus marginal cost as a percent of price. In practice it is constructed by subtracting the following from value of shipments: materials, supplies and containers, fuel, purchased electric energy, contract work, and payroll [Collins and Preston (1969)]. The residual, which is essentially value added minus payroll, is then divided by value of shipments. The advantages of this measure are that it can be constructed at the four-digit level and it avoids the accounting problems inherent in profit data.

The major drawback to the price-cost margin is that it still contains some marginal costs such as advertising and central office expenditures. The advertising-sales ratio controls for the advertising expenditures in the margin and proxies the product differentiation barrier to entry. Entrants into an industry where advertising is important must accept a lower price for their product or engage in massive advertising to offset their disadvantage. The output of the mid-point industry plant as a percent of industry value of shipments is a measure of the economies-of-scale barrier to entry. As the percent of industry output produced by a plant of minimum efficient scale increases, so does the displacement effect of a new firm. The industry capital-output ratio controls for the ratio of fixed to marginal costs. The more capital intensive the production process, the greater is the price-cost margin. The growth rate of industry value of shipments captures the effect on price-cost margins of unanticipated increases in industry demand or decreases in industry production costs.

The variables of primary interest in this equation are the concentration ratio and the measure of horizontal interdependence. These variables proxy the oligopolistic interdependence which is hypothesized to result from both fewness of sellers (CR) and interindustry contacts between those sellers (IHI). As oligopolistic interdependence increases, so should the ability of an industry's firms to effectively collude and obtain higher price-cost margins.

One final issue concerns the functional relationship between these two measures of firm interdependence and price-cost margins. As Weiss has noted, this is an area on which oligopoly models have not shed much light [Weiss (1975)].

> Where [oligopoly models] disagree is on the precise
> relation between concentration and prices. Bain and
> Chamberlin point to some critical level of concentration,
> Cournot and Stigler suggest that margins rise at an
> increasing rate with concentration, and most of the other
> theories might be interpreted to imply that margins rise
> in a fairly continuous way with concentration. This
> kind of question can't be resolved by theory. They
> are issues for empirical study. [Weiss (1975, p. 15)]

Based on previous work that the author did with Leonard Weiss, the concentration ratio will be introduced linearly in the price-cost margin equation. These concentration ratios will, however, understate the true degree of seller concentration if the relevant geographic market is local or regional instead of national. Collins and Preston's index of geographic dispersion of industrial activity is inserted to control for this deficiency of national concentration ratios.

Since there is no prior information about the relationship between the measures of horizontal interdependence and price-cost margins, two different functional forms will be estimated -- linear and quadratic. The linear specification assumes that margins increase at a constant rate with horizontal interdependence, while the quadratic specification permits margins to increase at either an increasing or decreasing rate with horizontal interdependence.

B. Advertising Equation

Cable has shown that the optimal advertising intensity (advertising expenditures as a percent of sales) for a profit maximizing monopolist is equal to the advertising elasticity of demand divided by the price elasticity of demand [Cable (1972)]. This optimality condition suggests an inverted-U relationship between advertising intensity and concentration. Initially, concentration increases the optimal advertising level by decreasing the price elasticity of the firm's demand curve. But, advertising may decrease at very high levels of concentration as firms collude in order to control offsetting advertising. At the extreme, a monopolist would advertise less since it would not face any offsetting advertising by competitors.

Several variables are included in this equation to control for

the effectiveness of advertising. Probably the most important of
these is consumer demand as a percent of total industry demand.
Advertising should be more effective in increasing demand, the
more consumer oriented is the industry's output. The product
durability dummy variable controls for differences in advertising
effectiveness due to product durability [Comanor and Wilson (1974)],
while the growth variable captures increased advertising effectiveness due to buyer turnover [Cable (1972), Comanor and Wilson
(1974) and Greer (1971)].

Finally, the price-cost margin variable is included in the
advertising equation since advertising expenses are included in
the margin and part of advertising expenditures may be considered
discretionary profits [Williamson (1963b)]. Also, advertising will
be more profitable, the greater the profit margin per unit sold
[Schmalensee (1972)].

As noted in Chapter I, horizontal interdependence may affect
non-price, as well as price, competition. If firm interdependence
is high, firms may channel their aggressive inclinations to non-
price areas such as advertising. Alternatively, firm interdependence may be so substantial that it even lessens non-price
competition, though this seems unlikely given the long lead times
and unpredictable payoffs of advertising campaigns. To control for
the possible impact of horizontal interdependence on advertising
intensity, it will be included in the advertising equation. As
in the margin equation, both linear and quadratic functional forms

will be estimated.

C. Concentration Equation

The level of industry concentration is hypothesized to be primarily a function of economies of scale. The minimum efficient scale variable captures production economies of scale, while the advertising-sales ratio controls for possible economies in advertising. As the output of an optimal scale plant increases relative to total industry output, the industry can support fewer efficient firms and concentration will necessarily increase.

The measure of horizontal interdependence is also included in the concentration equation. Large diversified firms might increase concentration through reciprocal dealing, predation and cross-subsidization, though it is not clear that the potential to engage in those practices is captured by the measure of horizontal interdependence. In any event, the concentration equation will be estimated controlling for the influence of horizontal interdependence.

The above arguments outline the theoretical basis for the hypothesized interrelationships among advertising, concentration and price-cost margins. Advertising is hypothesized to affect both concentration and price-cost margins, while they in turn are hypothesized to affect advertising intensity. In addition, concentration may influence price-cost margins. Based on these interrelationships, these three variables are treated as endogenous variables in a simultaneous equations system consisting of

equations (1), (2) and (3). The structural parameters of this
system will be estimated using a two-stage least squares (2SLS)
estimation technique.

Based on economic theory and the results of previous studies
[Cable (1972), Collins and Preston (1969)], the coefficients for
all of the exogenous variables, except for the measures of horizontal interdependence and geographic dispersion of industrial
activity, should be positive. The geographic dispersion variable
is constructed in such a fashion that a negative relationship is
expected between it and price-cost margins. In the margin equation,
the expected effect of horizontal interdependence is positive,
although one of the coefficients may be negative if a quadratic
function is used. In the advertising equation, the effect of horizontal interdependence is ambiguous while it may be positively
related to concentration. With respect to the endogenous variables,
advertising, price-cost margin, and concentration should have
positive coefficients except for the quadratic concentration term.
This term must be negative in order to give an inverted-U
relationship between advertising and concentration.

II. The Sample

The sample consists of 408 of the 417 four-digit Standard
Industrial Classification (S.I.C.) manufacturing industries from
the 1963 Census of Manufactures. Of the nine industries deleted
from the sample, two (2819, 3943) were dropped since advertising
data was not available. The seven other industries (2814, 3332,

3334, 3492, 3636, 3723, 3942) could not be used since the Census's disclosure requirement prevented the publication of four-firm concentration ratios.

The sample variables are defined in this chapter's appendix. The IHI measures were computed using the estimated market shares of the 195 sample firms in Chapter III. As noted earlier in Chapter II, the measures of horizontal interdependence are identical except for the assumption about the elasticity of the firms' demand curves. IHI1 was constructed assuming that $\eta = 0$, while η was $-1/2$, -1 and -2 for IHI2, IHI3, IHI4 respectively. Descriptive statistics for these measures and the rest of the sample variables are presented in Table VI.

The values of IHI range from a common minimum of zero to maximums of from .6858 (IHI4) to 1.2898 (IHI1). As expected, the numerical value of IHI is greater, the less elastic the firm's demand curve. Table VII presents more detailed information on the values of IHI1 across the sample industries. In 128 industries there is no horizontal interdependence. IHI equals zero for one of two reasons. Either the sample firms do not produce in that industry, or, if they do, they do not have any horizontal contacts outside that industry. The first reason applies to sixty-three industries and the second to sixty-five.

Table VI

Descriptive Statistics for Sample Variables

N = 408

Variable	Mean	Standard Deviation	Minimum	Maximum
M	.2486	.0836	.0308	.6080
AD	.0136	.0219	.0004	.2570
CR	.3767	.2139	.0400	.9700
IHI1	.1087	.1852	.0000	1.2898
IHI2	.0962	.1633	.0000	1.0520
IHI3	.0838	.1417	.0000	.9119
IHI4	.0589	.1007	.0000	.6858
KO	.3536	.2423	.0281	1.9890
CD	.2494	.3221	.0000	.9950
GR	.0398	.0373	-.0676	.2375
MES	.0232	.0347	.0000	.3110
GD	56.2700	32.8200	1.5440	157.0000
DUR	.5441	.4987	.0000	1.0000

Table VII

Distribution of Sample Industries by Values of IHI1

	Number of Industries	Percentage of Industries
.0000-.0500	247	60.5
.0501-.1000	42	10.3
.1001-.1500	18	4.4
.1501-.2000	17	4.2
.2001-.2500	19	4.4
.2501-.3000	12	2.9
.3001-.3500	12	2.9
.3501-.4000	12	2.9
.4001-.4500	7	1.7
.4501-.5000	1	.2
.5001-.5500	5	1.2
.5501-.6000	4	1.0
.6001-.6500	1	.2
.6501-.7000	3	.7
.7001+	8	2.0
Total	408	100.0

The values of IHI1 indicate the degree of horizontal interdependence among an industry's firms due to horizontal relationships in other industries. Since this measure is based on interactions outside the "home" industry, there is no unique market
structure associated with each value of industry horizontal
interdependence. For example, 2814, (Cyclic (Coal Tar) Crudes) and
3429 (Hardware, N.E.C.) have approximately the same values for
IHI1 -- .0923 and .0984 respectively. But, the market structures
in the two industries are very different. There are 5 sample
firms with a combined market share of .9475 in 2814 while the same
figures in 3429 are 7 and .1074. By definition, however, the
same values for IHI1 indicate that the level of horizontal interdependence due to external contacts is the same in both industries.

The maximum value of IHI1 exceeds one, 1.2898, and occurs
in industry 2131 -- Chewing and Smoking Tobacco. At first glance
this is a somewhat surprising result since the tobacco companies
are some of the least diversified firms in the sample. But they
do meet in one very important industry outside of this one -- 2111,
Cigarettes. The contacts in the cigarette industry, which accounts
for most of the firms' sales, creates a very strong degree of
horizontal interdependence among those firms. Thus, horizontal
interdependence from external contacts is high when firms meet
in an industry which is peripheral to their common "home" industry.

An interesting statistic which falls out of the procedures used
in computing horizontal interdependence is the absolute number of

interactions among the sample firms. This information is presented
in Table VIII. At the lower end, American Tobacco and P. Lorillard
each competed with only four other top 200 sample firms. At the
other extreme, General Electric was a direct competitor with 160
of the other 194 sample firms. The number of contacts per direct
competitor ranged from 1.00 (Gulf Oil, Mack Trucks, Richfield Oil,
Sunray DX Oil) to 5.74 (General Motors) and 5.94 (General Electric).
All in all, an average sample firm competed with an average of 76.3
sample firms and had an average of 2.34 contacts with each of those
firms.

The correlation matrix for the sample variables is presented
in Table IX. The simple correlations between the endogenous
variables (M, CR and AD) are all positive and significant at the
one percent level. Not surprisingly, the simple correlations
between the four measures of horizontal interdependence are large,
ranging from .962 to .999, and significant at the one percent
level. They are also significantly correlated with concentration,
but not with advertising or price-cost margin.

III. Empirical Results

Before examining the empirical results, it is necessary to
discuss two estimation issues raised by the specification of
the simultaneous equation system in Section I. The first issue
deals with the identification of the three equations. The order
condition for identifiability indicates that all three equations
are overidentified and we can therefore obtain consistent estimates

Table VIII

Distribution of Firms by Number of Sample Firm Competitors

Number of Competitors	Number of Firms	Percentage of Firms
0-20	14	7.2
21-40	25	12.8
41-60	24	12.3
61-80	44	22.6
81-100	33	16.9
101-120	25	12.8
121-140	21	10.8
141-160	9	4.6
Total	195	100.0

Table IX

Correlation Matrix For Sample Variables

	M	AD	CR	IHI1	IHI2	IHI3	IHI4	KO	CD	GR	MES
M	1.000										
AD	.448	1.000									
CR	.336	.163	1.000								
IHI1	.012	.013	.231	1.000							
IHI2	.004	.007	.228	.999	1.000						
IHI3	-.008	-.001	.223	.995	.998	1.000					
IHI4	-.045	-.028	.204	.962	.973	.984	1.000				
KO	.350	-.089	.291	.202	.195	.185	.151	1.000			
CD	.037	.401	-.051	-.194	-.197	-.201	-.208	-.382	1.000		
GR	.166	.118	-.005	.106	.106	.107	.105	.026	-.032	1.000	
MES	.189	.065	.686	.110	.108	.104	.089	.136	-.007	-.077	1.000
GD	-.010	.022	.124	-.030	-.030	-.029	-.027	-.045	.183	-.056	.155
DUR	.037	-.159	.055	.013	.017	.023	.041	.032	-.343	-.022	.107

Table IX (continued)

	GD	DUR
GD	1.000	
DUR	-.188	1.000

of the structural parameters. The second issue arises since the three-equation system is linear in parameters but nonlinear in endogenous variables -- the squared concentration term in the advertising equation. As a result, the reduced form equations are functions of the square root of linear relations among the exogenous variables. And, unless the structural parameters are known, the exact form of the reduced form equations will not be. The reduced form equations can, however, be approximated by a polynomial function of the exogenous variables [Kelejian (1971)]. This will produce consistent estimates of the system's parameters using two-stage least squares estimation techniques. This thesis uses second-degree polynomials to approximate the system's reduced form equations.

Another relevant issue concerns the correct interpretation of the coefficients of the IHI variables. As noted earlier, these measures of horizontal interdependence capture all of the external contacts among the 195 sample firms in a given industry. By definition these measures omit any contacts with the five top 200 firms which were dropped from the sample (see Chapter III), as well as any diversified firms outside of the top 200. These data limitations will tend to understate the degree of horizontal interdependence which exists in the population of all diversified firms. As a result, the statistical results in this chapter should be interpreted with respect to only the 195 sample firms.

The three equations of the model were initially estimated

using ordinary least squares (OLS) regressions. This was done

for two reasons. First, OLS regressions provide an inexpensive

means for examining the sensitivity of the regression results

to the different measures of IHI. Secondly, the OLS estimates can

later be compared to the 2SLS estimates to determine the extent

of simultaneous equations bias.

The OLS estimates of the price-cost margin equation for all

four measures of IHI are presented in Table X. The margin

equation was estimated without the IHI measures, equation (i), and

with the measures introduced in a linear and quadratic fashion,

equations (ii) and (iii) respectively. With respect to equation

(i), the results are consistent with previous work of the author.

Advertising, concentration, capital-output ratio and growth all

have significant, positive relationships with price-cost margin.

The advertising coefficient significantly exceeds one, indicating

that advertising has an impact on margins over and above that due

to its inclusion in the margin. As expected, geographic dispersion

is significantly negatively related to margins. The coefficient

of the minimum efficient scale variable is not significantly

different from zero.

The surprising feature of these results is that the measures

of horizontal interdependence consistently have significant

negative relationships with price-cost margins. Moreover, these

negative relationships hold for both the linear and quadratic

functional forms and are insensitive to the particular measure

Table X

OLS Estimates of Price-Cost Margin Equation (1)

Equation	(i)	IHI1		IHI2	
		(ii)	(iii)	(ii)	(iii)
CONSTANT	.1683	.1681	.1689	.1682	.1692
	(17.15)	(17.32)	(17.75)	(17.35)	(17.76)
AD	1.6536	1.6435	1.6093	1.6400	1.6133
	(11.00)	(11.05)	(11.02)	(11.03)	(11.04)
CR	.0629	.0746	.0849	.0750	.0849
	(2.89)	(3.42)	(3.94)	(3.44)	(3.94)
KO	.1123	.1180	.1241	.1178	.1237
	(8.03)	(8.46)	(9.01)	(8.45)	(8.99)
MES	.0686	.0513	.0281	.0501	.0276
	(0.54)	(0.41)	(0.23)	(0.40)	(0.22)
GR	.2255	.2532	.3169	.2543	.3136
	(2.61)	(2.95)	(3.70)	(2.96)	(3.66)
GD	-.0003	-.0003	-.0003	-.0003	-.0003
	(-2.90)	(-3.05)	(-3.42)	(-3.06)	(-3.43)
IHI	-----	-.0501	-.2014	-.0652	-.2303
		(-3.15)	(-5.12)	(-3.24)	(-5.02)
IHI^2	-----	-----	.1991	-----	.2620
			(4.12)		(3.99)
R^2	.402	.416	.440	.417	.439
d.f.	401	400	399	400	399

Figures in parentheses are t-ratios

Table X (continued)

Equation	IHI3		IHI4	
	(ii)	(iii)	(ii)	(iii)
CONSTANT	.1684 (17.38)	.1695 (17.77)	.1691 (17.49)	.1700 (17.73)
AD	1.6345 (11.00)	1.6184 (11.06)	1.6172 (10.89)	1.6181 (10.99)
CR	.0754 (3.46)	.0845 (3.92)	.0764 (3.51)	.0824 (3.80)
KO	.1175 (8.45)	.1231 (8.94)	.1161 (8.39)	.1203 (8.72)
MES	.0485 (0.38)	.0280 (0.22)	.0439 (0.35)	.0311 (0.25)
GR	.2555 (2.98)	.3075 (3.59)	.2584 (3.02)	.2891 (3.38)
GD	-.0003 (-3.06)	-.0003 (-3.41)	-.0003 (-3.06)	-.0003 (-3.30)
IHI	-.0773 (-3.34)	-.2603 (-4.83)	-.1161 (-3.60)	-.3070 (-4.12)
IHI^2	-----	.3410 (3.74)	-----	.5052 (2.83)
R^2	.418	.438	.420	.432
d.f.	400	399	400	399

of horizontal interdependence employed. These results are the
complete opposite of the positive relationship predicted by the
mutual forbearance hypothesis.

The OLS estimates of the advertising equation are presented
in Table XI. As in the margin equation, all four measures of IHI
were introduced in both a linear, equation (v), and quadratic,
equation (vi), functional form. In equation (iv) the advertising
equation was estimated without the IHI variables. As expected,
price-cost margin, concentration and consumer demand all have
significant positive relationships with advertising. Growth has
a non-significant positive coefficient, while that for product
durability is negative and also non-significant.

When the measures of horizontal interdependence are introduced
linearly in equation (v), the coefficients are all positive,
though non-significant. In the quadratic form, equation (vi),
the linear term is positive and significantly so for three of
the measures, while the squared term is negative and non-significant
for all four of the measures.

OLS estimates for the third equation of the model, concentration, are listed in Table XII. Not surprisingly, minimum efficient
scale has a very substantial, positive relationship with concentration. Advertising also has a significant positive relationship
with concentration, suggesting that there are economies of scale
in advertising. All four measures of horizontal interdependence
have significant positive relationships with concentration.

Table XI

OLS Estimates of Advertising Equation (2)

| Equation | (iv) | IHI1 | | IHI2 | |
		(v)	(vi)	(v)	(vi)
CONSTANT	-.0314	-.0317	-.0331	-.0318	-.0331
	(-7.45)	(-7.53)	(-7.76)	(-7.54)	(-7.77)
M	.1123	.1135	.1164	.1137	.1164
	(9.84)	(9.94)	(10.12)	(9.94)	(10.13)
CR	.0554	.0522	.0524	.0523	.0526
	(3.56)	(3.33)	(3.35)	(3.34)	(3.37)
CR^2	-.0568	-.0550	-.0568	-.0550	-.0569
	(-3.39)	(-3.28)	(-3.39)	(-3.28)	(-3.40)
GR	.0387	.0345	.0255	.0346	.0257
	(1.64)	(1.46)	(1.05)	(1.46)	(1.06)
IHI	-----	.0072	.0258	.0080	.0302
		(1.46)	(2.29)	(1.43)	(2.30)
IHI^2	-----	-----	-.0252	-----	-.0347
			(-1.83)		(-1.87)
CD	.0257	.0265	.0276	.0265	.0276
	(8.95)	(9.08)	(9.29)	(9.07)	(9.29)
DUR	-.0021	-.0019	-.0017	-.0019	-.0017
	(-1.11)	(-1.01)	(-0.92)	(-1.02)	(-0.91)
R^2	.374	.378	.383	.377	.383
d.f.	401	400	399	400	399

Figures in parentheses are t-ratios

Table XI (continued)

Equation	IHI3		IHI4	
	(v)	(vi)	(v)	(vi)
CONSTANT	-.0318	-.0331	-.0319	-.0327
	(-7.14)	(-7.76)	(-7.54)	(-7.69)
M	.1138	.1162	.1141	.1153
	(9.94)	(10.12)	(9.93)	(10.02)
CR	.0524	.0528	.0529	.0530
	(3.34)	(3.38)	(3.38)	(3.39)
CR^2	-.0551	-.0570	-.0554	-.0567
	(-3.28)	(-3.40)	(-3.30)	(-3.38)
GR	.0346	.0263	.0349	.0296
	(1.46)	(1.09)	(1.47)	(1.23)
IHI	.0090	.0349	.0112	.0407
	(1.39)	(2.28)	(1.23)	(1.94)
IHI^2	-----	-.0478	-----	-.0774
		(-1.86)		(-1.56)
CD	.0265	.0275	.0264	.0270
	(9.06)	(9.28)	(9.03)	(9.17)
DUR	-.0019	-.0017	-.0020	-.0017
	(-1.03)	(-0.90)	(-1.23)	(-0.93)
R^2	.377	.383	.377	.380
d.f.	400	399	400	399

TABLE XII

OLS Estimates of Concentration Equation (3)

Equation	(vii)	IHI1 (viii)	IHI2 (viii)	IHI3 (viii)	IHI4 (viii)
Constant	.2638 (25.93)	.2468 (23.16)	.2466 (23.10)	.2464 (23.02)	.2466 (22.88)
AD	1.1613 (3.33)	1.1522 (3.38)	1.1616 (3.40)	1.1736 (3.44)	1.2104 (3.54)
MES	4.1852 (18.99)	4.0792 (18.82)	4.0818 (18.83)	4.0857 (18.85)	4.1018 (18.91)
IHI	......	.1804 (4.46)	.2040 (4.44)	.2333 (4.41)	.3143 (4.22)
R^2	.485	.509	.509	.509	.507
d.f.	405	404	404	404	404

Figures in parentheses are t-ratios

The three-equation model was next estimated using a two-stage least squares (2SLS) estimation technique. The 2SLS estimates of the model's structural parameters are presented in Table XIII. Since the measures of horizontal interdependence were so highly correlated, the model was estimated for only one of the measures -- IHI1. The simple correlations between IHI1 and the other measures range from .962 - .999.

In the price-cost margin equation, the 2SLS estimates for the exogenous variables are generally very similar to the OLS estimates. The one exception is the minimum efficient scale (MES) variable whose 2SLS coefficient estimates substantially exceed its OLS estimates. The significant negative relationship between IHI1 and price-cost margins is essentially unchanged, both with respect to the magnitude of the coefficients and their level of significance. As before, this relationship is more significant for the quadratic functional form than for the linear.

With respect to the endogenous variables, the 2SLS estimates are sensitive to the specification of the margin equation. The coefficient for concentration is much smaller when IHI1 is introduced linearly than when it is introduced in a quadratic fashion. The opposite situation holds for the advertising variable, whose coefficients significantly exceed one at the ten percent level for a one-tailed test. The reduction in concentration's coefficient is apparently offset by the substantial increase in the coefficient for minimum efficient scale. These two variables are highly

TABLE XIII

2SLS Estimates of Three-Equation Model

Dependent Variable	M	M	AD	AD	CR
Constant	.1782 (15.53)	.1753 (15.61)	-.0254 (-3.48)	-.0270 (-3.67)	.2408 (19.38)
AD	1.5436 (5.40)	1.3901 (4.93)	.....	.....	1.6284 (2.65)
CR	.0283 (0.70)	.0651 (1.60)	.0905 (2.51)	.0888 (2.49)	.....
CR^2	.....	.....	-.0865 (-2.32)	-.0869 (-2.35)	.....
KO	.1244 (8.06)	.1250 (8.29)	.....	.....	.....
MES	.2408 (1.32)	.1187 (0.66)	.....	.....	4.0598 (18.67)
GR	.2683 (3.07)	.3358 (3.86)	.0626 (2.37)	.0543 (2.00)	.....
GD	-.0003 (-2.92)	-.0003 (-3.35)	.....	.....	.....
IHI1	-.0494 (-2.69)	-.1966 (-4.81)	.0040 (0.74)	.0165 (1.34)	.1801 (4.45)
$IHI1^2$	.....	.1968 (4.01)	.....	-.0165 (-1.12)	.....
M	.....	.....	.0485 (1.97)	.0561 (2.22)	.....
CD	.....	.....	.0276 (9.05)	.0283 (9.19)	.....
DUR	.....	.....	-.0014 (-0.74)	-.0013 (-0.70)	.....

Figures in parentheses are t-ratios.

correlated and their relative significance is very sensitive to
the specification of the margin equation.

Given this significant negative relationship between price-
cost margins and horizontal interdependence, it is of interest to
determine the relative importance of this relationship compared
to the relationships between margins and such traditional elements
of market structure as concentration and advertising. This can
be done by computing the elasticity of price-cost margins with
respect to these different variables using their mean values. The
elasticity for IHI1 is -.022 in the linear case and -.067 in
the quadratic case. The corresponding figures are .043 and .099
for concentration and .084 and .076 for advertising. These
elasticities indicate that the relationship between IHI1 and
margins is of a rather small order of magnitude in the linear
case, but not in the quadratic case where the elasticity of IHI1
approaches those of concentration and advertising.

One final issue concerns the possibility that in the quadratic
case IHI1 might have a positive influence on price-cost margins
over some range of values. This can occur since the coefficient
of the squared term is positive and dominates the negative linear
term when IHI1 exceeds 0.9990. After examining the data, however,
it appears that the positive-sloped portion of this function results
from the quadratic functional form imposed on the data and should
not be taken too seriously. 94.9% of the observations lie on
the negative-sloped portion of this curve, while only two of the

408 industries have values of IHI1 sufficient to create a positive effect on margins. Those two industries are 2131 (Chewing and Smoking Tobacco) and 3729 (Aircraft Equipment, N.E.C.) whose values of IHI1 are 1.2898 and 1.1380 respectively.

The 2SLS estimates of the advertising equation are consistent with prior expectations and don't present any surprises. Price-cost margins, concentration, growth and consumer demand all have significant positive relationships with advertising, while the coefficient for product durability is negative and non-significant. The relationship between IHI1 and advertising, though still positive, is now insignificant for both the linear and quadratic functional forms. This is reflected in the elasticity of advertising with respect to IHI1 which is .032 in the linear case and .103 in the quadratic. These figures are miniscule when compared to the corresponding figures for concentration, .702 and .646, and price-cost margins, .887 and 1.025.

In the third equation of the model, advertising, minimum efficient scale and horizontal interdependence all have significant positive relationships with industry concentration. The results for advertising and minimum efficient scale are consistent with prior expectations, while there really wasn't any strong pre-disposition concerning the relationship between concentration and horizontal interdependence. The only theoretical rationale dealt with the prospect of diversified firms increasing concentration by engaging in such practices as reciprocity, predation and cross-subsidization. Though, it is not clear that the measure of horizontal interdependence adequately captures the potential of the sample firms to use those practices. A more likely explanation is that the sample firms produce in concentrated industries and this presence produces the significant positive association between concentration and horizontal interdependence.

The relative strength of this relationship can, however, be examined by computing the elasticity of concentration with respect to these three explanatory variables. As before, all of the elasticities were computed using the mean values of the variables. The elasticity for horizontal interdependence is .052 which is close to that for advertising, .059. But both of these are considerably less than the elasticity for minimum efficient scale, .250, which indicates that a one hundred percent increase in minimum efficient scale will be associated with a twenty-five percent increase in concentration.

In Chapter III it was noted that the diversification activities of the sample firms could be characterized as diversification with more breadth than depth. This finding raises the interesting question of whether firm interdependence is a function of the depth of interfirm contacts, as captured by the elasticity measures of horizontal interdependence, or is simply a function of the number of these contacts. In order to test this "breadth versus depth" issue, two measures were constructed which capture only the number, and not relative importance, of horizontal contacts between sample firms. These two measures were defined as follows:

$$AC_k = \sum_m MS_{mk} \cdot AC_{mk}$$

$$TC_k = \sum_m MS_{mk} \cdot TC_{mk}$$

where MS_{mk} is the market share of the mth sample firm in the kth industry, AC_{mk} is the average number of horizontal contacts that the mth firm had with other sample firms in this industry, and TC_{mk} is simply the total number of those contacts. Thus, AC captures the average number of contacts a firm had with its competitors in a given industry, while TC just looks at the total number of those contacts.

These two measures of interfirm contacts were introduced in both a linear, equation (ii), and quadratic, equation (iii), fashion in the price-cost margin equation. The 2SLS estimates for these equations are presented in Table XIV. These two measures have non-significant negative relationships with price-cost margins in both the linear and quadratic cases. The implication of these results is that firm interdependence is a function of both the number of interfirm contacts and the relative importance of those contacts to the firms involved.

One final issue concerns the relationship between firm diversification and horizontal interdependence. These variables are related since firm diversification creates the interindustry contacts which form the basis for horizontal interdependence among

TABLE XIV

2SLS Estimates of Price-Cost Margin Equation (1)

Equation	(ii)	(iii)	(ii)	(iii)
Constant	.1735	.1712	.1747	.1751
	(15.25)	(14.88)	(14.97)	(15.00)
AD	1.5276	1.4937	1.5768	1.5914
	(5.17)	(5.05)	(5.48)	(5.53)
CR	.0482	.0724	.0345	.0350
	(1.15)	(1.55)	(0.84)	(0.85)
KO	.1167	.1171	.1182	.1198
	(7.65)	(7.70)	(7.65)	(7.68)
MES	.1824	.0718	.1906	.1959
	(1.07)	(0.37)	(1.03)	(1.06)
GR	.2507	.2646	.2476	.2509
	(2.83)	(2.97)	(2.77)	(2.80)
GD	-.0003	-.0003	-.0003	-.0003
	(-2.94)	(-3.11)	(-2.84)	(-2.91)
AC	-.0023	-.0076	.....	.....
	(-0.90)	(-1.47)		
AC^2	.....	.0007	.....	.....
		(1.17)		
TC	.....	.....	-.0001	-.0003
			(-0.52)	(-0.90)
TC^2	.....	.....	.....	.000002
				(0.74)

Figures in parentheses are t-ratios.

firms. This relationship raises the issue of whether or not it
is possible to distinguish between the effects of firm diversification per se and horizontal interdependence in a cross-section
analysis of price-cost margins. It might be the case that the
measure of horizontal interdependence is simply proxying firm
diversification and not the unique influence of interindustry
contacts.

In order to statistically examine this issue, the following
measure was constructed to reflect the diversified nature of
the sample firms for each industry in which they produced.

$$BI_k = \sum_m MS_{mk} \cdot BI_m$$

where MS_{mk} is the market share of the mth firm in the kth industry
and BI_m is the value of the Berry index for the mth firm.

The relationship between horizontal interdependence and price-
cost margins was reestimated reestimated including BI, which is highly
correlated with IHI1(.667). The 2SLS estimates for this specification
of the price-cost margin equation are presented in Table XV.
These results indicate that horizontal interdependence still has
a negative relationship with price-cost margins after controlling
for firm diversification, though this relationship is no longer
significant in the linear case. The coefficient for BI is non-
significant in both equations. Thus, when the degree of firm
diversification is held constant, the relationship between
horizontal interdependence remains negative, but only significantly
so in the quadratic functional form.

TABLE XV

2SLS Estimates of Price-Cost Margin Equation (1)

Equation	(ix)	(x)
Constant	.1677 (14.18)	.1766 (14.92)
AD	1.4806 (5.16)	1.4000 (4.94)
CR	.0911 (1.89)	.0547 (1.13)
KO	.1198 (8.00)	.1215 (8.24)
MES	.0361 (0.19)	.1167 (0.64)
GR	.2793 (3.18)	.3281 (3.76)
GD	-.0003 (-3.17)	-.0003 (-3.12)
BI	-.0380 (-0.99)	.0409 (0.97)
IHI1	-.0375 (-1.55)	-.2388 (-4.41)
$IHI1^2$	.....	.2263 (4.14)

Figures in parentheses are t-ratios.

IV. Conclusion

The results in this chapter do not support the mutual forbearance hypothesis. Horizontal interdependence consistently
has a negative relationship with industry price-cost margins. This
relationship is, however, only significant when the measures of
horizontal interdependence capture both the breadth and depth of
interfirm contacts. When a measure of firm diversification is
introduced into the margin equation, horizontal interdependence
is still negatively related to margins, but the relationship is
only significant in the quadratic case.

One possible explanation of this unexpected negative relationship between margins and horizontal interdependence is that the
mutual forbearance hypothesis ignores the costs of reaching multi-
market collusive agreements. The logistics of arranging such
agreements may be so complicated that firms pursue competitive
policies instead.

Finally, horizontal interdependence has a non-significant
positive relationship with advertising and a significant positive
relationship with concentration. The latter relationship presumably
reflects the fact that the sample firms tend to produce in concentrated industries.

APPENDIX C

Data Sources

The data used for industry value of shipments, minimum efficient scale, rate of growth, geographic dispersion, and price-cost margin all came from the 1963 Census of Manufactures. Industry value of shipments is measured in producer prices and includes the total shipments of establishments classified in an industry. The capital-output ratio is defined as the gross book value of assets as of December 31, 1962, divided by the 1963 value of shipments, where the book value of assets is from the Annual Survey of Manufactures: 1964-1965. The minimum efficient scale variable is the output of the industry mid-point plant as a percent of that industry's value of shipments. Collins and Preston define their index of geographic dispersion as "the sum of the absolute differences between the percentage of value added accounted for by establishments in each [census] region and the percentage of total manufacturing value added accounted for by that region." [Collins and Preston (1969, p. 286)]. The rate of growth in industry demand is the average annual rate of growth of industry value of shipments from 1954 to 1963.

The industry price-cost margin approximates the Lerner index of monopoly power -- price minus marginal cost as a percent of price. In practice it is constructed by subtracting from value of shipments the following: materials, supplies and containers, fuel, purchased energy, contract work, and payroll. The residual, which is essentially value added minus payroll, is then divided by value of shipments [Collins and Preston (1969)].

The concentration ratios came from Concentration Ratios in Manufacturing Industry -- 1963, which is published by the Senate Committee on the Judiciary. The four-firm concentration ratio is defined as the percent of industry value of shipments shipped by the industry's four largest firms.

The advertising and consumer demand variables were derived from the Office of Business Economics' 1963 input-output tables. The advertising variable is the direct requirements coefficient of each manufacturing sector for inputs from the sector labeled "advertising." Industry consumer demand is "personal consumption expenditures" divided by "total output," where both figures are from the transactions matrix of the input-output tables. Finally, durable goods industries were assigned a value of one and non-durables a value of zero based on Leonard Weiss' judgment.

CHAPTER V

Vertical Interdependence and Industry Price-Cost Margins

The relationship between horizontal interdependence and
industry price-cost margins was examined in Chapter IV. In this
chapter the analysis focuses on the firm interdependence created
by vertical relationships between firms. The measures of vertical
buyer and seller interdependence derived in Chapter II are estimated
for the 195 sample firms. These measures are then introduced
as additional explanatory variables in the three-equation model
of the determinants of industry price-cost margins.

I.   The Model

The relationship between vertical interdependence and industry
price-cost margins is estimated using the three-equation simultaneous equations system developed in Chapter IV. The three equations of that model are reproduced below with y's once again
denoting endogenous variables and x's exogenous variables.

(1) $$y_1 = \alpha_1 + \gamma_{12}y_2 + \gamma_{13}y_3 + \beta_{11}x_1 + \beta_{12}x_2 + \beta_{13}x_3 + \beta_{14}x_4$$
$$+ \beta_{15}x_5$$

(2) $$y_2 = \alpha_2 + \gamma_{21}y_1 + \gamma_{23}y_3 + \gamma_{24}y_3^2 + \beta_{23}x_3 + \beta_{25}x_5 + \beta_{26}x_6$$
$$+ \beta_{27}x_7$$

(3) $\qquad y_3 = \alpha_3 + \gamma_{32}y_2 + \beta_{32}x_2 + \beta_{35}x_5$

where:

$\qquad y_1$ = industry price-cost margin (M)

$\qquad y_2$ = industry advertising-sales ratio (AD)

$\qquad y_3$ = industry four-firm concentration ratio (CR)

$\qquad x_1$ = industry capital-output ratio (KO)

$\qquad x_2$ = output of mid-point plant as a percent of industry output (MES)

$\qquad x_3$ = rate of growth of industry value of shipments (GR)

$\qquad x_4$ = Collins and Preston index of geographic dispersion of industry industrial activity (GD)

$\qquad x_5$ = industry vertical buyer interdependence (VBI) industry vertical seller interdependence (VSI)

$\qquad x_6$ = ratio of consumer demand to total industry demand (CD)

$\qquad x_7$ = product durability dummy variable (DUR)

This model is identical to the one estimated in Chapter IV, except for the substitution of the measures of vertical interdependence for the measure of horizontal interdependence. The theoretical rationale for their inclusion in the model is discussed below. With respect to the other explanatory variables, the general specification of the three-equation model was discussed in Chapter IV and, consequently, will not be repeated here.

The measures of vertical interdependence are designed to capture the firm interdependence created by vertical relationships among competitors in a given industry (See Chapter II for a more detailed discussion). A firm can have two types of vertical relationships with a competitor: buyer and seller. In the buyer case, vertical interdependence results from the prospect that a competitor will stop selling inputs to another firm, thereby foreclosing that firm from an input source. The measure of industry vertical buyer interdependence (VBI) proxies the firm interdependence hypothesized to be created by those buyer relationships among an industry's firms. In the seller case, vertical interdependence results from the fear that a competitor will stop purchasing products from another firm, thereby reducing that firm's sales. The hypothesized interdependence from these seller relationships among an industry's firms is proxied by the measure of industry vertical seller interdependence (VSI). These two measures thus incorporate the influence of all possible vertical relationships which an industry's firms may have with one another.

The measures of vertical interdependence are introduced separately in the model (The joint effects of both vertical measures along with the horizontal measure are examined in Chapter VI). In the price-cost margin equation, each vertical measure is introduced in conjunction with the concentration ratio. This makes it possible to capture the oligopolistic interdependence arising from both the fewness of sellers (CR) and the vertical relationships among those sellers (VBI and VSI). As oligopolistic interdependence increases, so should the ability of an industry's firms to effectively collude and obtain higher margins.

As in the horizontal case, the effect of increased firm interdependence on advertising intensity is uncertain. Increased firm
interdependence due to vertical contacts may plausibly increase or
decrease advertising intensity. To the extent that it decreases
price competition among firms, it may lead to increased competition
in non-price areas such as advertising. On the other hand, if
firm interdependence is sufficiently large, it might even enable
firms to limit their competition in non-price areas as well.

The measures of vertical interdependence are also included in
the concentration equation. Large diversified firms might increase
concentration through reciprocal dealing, predation and cross-
subsidization, though it is not clear that those potentially
anticompetitive practices would be captured by the measures of
vertical interdependence.

As in the horizontal case, the relationships between the
measures of firm interdependence and price-cost margins and advertising will be estimated using both linear and quadratic functional forms. Vertical interdependence is expected to have a positive
relationship with price-cost margins, though one of the coefficients may be negative when the quadratic functional forms are
estimated. As noted above, the effect of vertical interdependence
on advertising intensity is ambiguous. If the measures of vertical
interdependence do capture those aspects of diversified firms
which are hypothesized to increase concentration, their coefficients
should be positive. Finally, the signs of the other variables'

coefficients are expected to be the same as in the previous
chapter.

II.   The Sample

The sample consists of the same 408 four-digit industries used
in Chapter IV. Since all of the sample variables are the same
except for the measures of vertical interdependence, only these
variables will be discussed in this section. The definitions
and data sources for the other variables are discussed in the
appendix to Chapter IV.

The measures of vertical buyer and seller interdependence
capture a firm's interdependence with a competitor due to its
vertical contacts with that competitor. Unfortunately, it was not
possible to determine the exact vertical relationships which
existed among the sample firms in 1963. Instead, the 1967 Input-
Output tables of the Department of Commerce were used to determine
"potential" vertical relationships among sample firms.[1] A firm
was considered to have a "potential" seller relationship with a
competitor if that competitor had a non-zero direct requirements
coefficient for one or more of that firm's products. The potential
nature of this relationship is stressed since there is no guarantee
that this firm actually fulfilled any of its competitor's input
requirements. A non-zero direct requirements coefficient merely
indicates that such a relationship is possible.

Given the industries in which a firm produced and the input
requirements of its competitors, it was possible to determine that

firm's potential sales to those competitors. And, since vertical

relationships are necessarily symmetric, those potential sales also

indicated potential purchases by those competitors. This information

could then be used to estimate both seller and buyer vertical inter-

dependence. Before estimating the measures of vertical inter-

dependence, however, it was necessary to deal with the problems

posed by firm integration.

The firm integration issue arose in two different contexts.

First, the direct requirements coefficient of an industry for its

own product was generally non-zero, though of a relatively small

order of magnitude. The rare exceptions were industries like primary

copper (3331) and motor vehicles and parts (3717) where it was

.31133 and .28027 respectively. Do these coefficients indicate

that firms in these industries used some of their output as an

input in their production processes? Or, were these firms simply

purchasing inputs from suppliers classified in the same industry?

In the latter case there is a vertical relationship with another

firm while in the former there is not. Secondly, if a firm pro-

duced in several industries, a plant in one industry may have

supplied inputs to plants classified in other industries. Alterna-

tively, that plant might have produced a seven-digit product

different from those required by the other plants from that industry.

Again, the latter situation creates a vertical relationship with

another firm, while the former does not.

The above situations indicate that a firm's potential vertical

relationships with other firms depend on the extent to which that firm is vertically integrated. As a firm becomes more integrated, its dependence on other firms for input supplies is reduced, thereby reducing its potential vertical interactions with those firms. In estimating the measures of vertical interdependence, it was thus necessary to make an assumption about firm integration.

The firm integration problem can be approached from the perspective of S.I.C. industry definitions. If an industry contains plants which produce homogeneous products, then firm integration can be assumed if a firm has a plant in that industry and also uses some of that industry's output as an input in its manufacturing operations. On the other hand, if the industry definition is broad and includes many different products, the output is heterogeneous and it is more difficult to assume firm integration. A firm might procure inputs from this industry, but not from its own plant since it does not produce the particular product required by the firm's other manufacturing operations. In short, the appropriateness of assuming firm integration (or ignoring it) depends on the industry definitions employed by the Bureau of the Census.

The solution adopted in this thesis was to estimate the measures of vertical interdependence using two different assumptions about the nature of industry output -- homogeneous and heterogeneous. Under the homogeneity assumption, a firm's input requirements from a given industry were "netted" of any internal production of that product by the firm. This assumption thus allows for firm integration, though undoubtedly overstating its extent by treating all seven-digit products within a four-digit industry as perfect

substitites. Under the heterogeneity assumption, a firm's input

requirements were determined purely by the input-output coefficients

and no adjustment was made for firm integration. This assumption

recognizes that seven-digit products may not be perfect substitutes

and that a firm may purchase products from other firms even when

it has plants classified in the same industry.

The importance of the firm integration issue can be seen in

Table XVI.   This table provides information on the number of

potential sales contacts a sample firm had with an average competi-

tor. This statistic was computed assuming both homogeneous

(assumption two) and heterogeneous output (assumption one). Not

surprisingly, a firm had fewer potential sales contacts with an

average competitor when that competitor had some integrated

operations (assumption two). When no firm integration is allowed

(assumption one), over seventy percent of the sample firms had

more than five potential sales contacts with each competitor. This

figure drops off to forty-four percent when firm integration is

allowed. Under both assumptions, General Electric had the

largest number of potential sales contacts per competitor --

37.33 under the first assumption and 21.71 under the second.

The descriptive statistics for the measures of vertical buyer

and seller interdependence, both unadjusted and adjusted for firm

integration, are presented in Table XVII. As expected, the measures

TABLE XVI

Distribution of Sample Firms by Number of Potential

Sales Contacts Per Sample Competitor

Number of Potential Sales Contacts Per Competitor	Number of Firms (Assumption One)	Number of Firms (Assumption Two)
0.00–1.00	4	24
1.01–2.00	14	18
2.01–3.00	14	27
3.01–4.00	12	19
4.01–5.00	13	21
5.01–6.00	19	26
6.01–7.00	13	13
7.01–8.00	8	10
8.01–9.00	19	9
9.01–10.00	13	6
10.01–11.00	12	5
11.01–12.00	8	4
12.01–13.00	6	3
13.01–14.00	11	3
14.01–15.00	6	2
15.01–16.00	6	2
16.01–17.00	2	2
17.01–18.00	1	0
18.01–19.00	1	0
19.01–20.00	2	0
20.01–21.00	1	0
21.01–22.00	2	1

Number of Potential Sales Contacts Per Competitor	Number of Firms (Assumption One)	Number of Firms (Assumption Two)
22.01-23.00	0	0
23.01-24.00	2	0
24.01+	6	0
Total	195	195

TABLE XVII

Descriptive Statistics for Measures of Vertical Interdependence

N=408

Measure	Mean	Standard Deviation	Minimum	Maximum
VSI	.4519	.9252	.0000	8.4616
AVSI	.0787	.1962	.0000	1.6802
VBI	.0135	.0276	.0000	.2347
AVBI	.0049	.0212	.0000	.3226

which were not adjusted for firm integration (VSI and VBI) generally
have larger values than those which were adjusted to account for
possible firm integration (AVSI and AVBI).[2] The adjustment for
firm integration tends to reduce vertical interdependence since a
firm's potential sales to and/or purchases from a competitor will
be reduced the more integrated the firm. A firm's potential sales
will be reduced since it is using the material internally and
this automatically lessens its potential purchases from other firms.
In essence, vertical integration lessens a firm's reliance on
vertical relationships with other firms -- a conclusion reached long
ago by American corporations.

The sensitivity of the measures to the integration adjustment
is further illustrated by the simple correlations between the
adjusted and unadjusted values. The correlation matrix for these
variables, as well as the rest of the sample variables, is presented
in Table XVIII. The simple correlation between VSI and AVSI is .494,
while it is .297 for VBI and AVBI. Also, the simple correlation
between AVSI and AVBI is .401, which is smaller than the .790
for VSI and VBI. With respect to the endogenous variables, VBI
and VSI are both significantly correlated with concentration at
the one-percent level, but not with advertising or price-cost
margins. AVBI is not significantly correlated with any of the
endogenous variables, while AVSI is significantly correlated with
concentration, but not with advertising or price-cost margins.

TABLE XVIII

Correlation Matrix for Sample Variables

	M	AD	CR	VSI	AVSI	VBI	AVBI	KO	CD	GR	MES	GD	DUR
M	1.000												
AD	.448	1.000											
CR	.336	.163	1.000										
VSI	.030	-.073	.126	1.000									
AVSI	.062	.132	.122	.494	1.000								
VBI	.004	-.088	.252	.790	.452	1.000							
AVBI	.041	.095	.074	.216	.401	.297	1.000						
KO	.350	-.089	.291	.187	.112	.253	.170	1.000					
CD	.037	.401	-.051	-.186	-.131	-.185	-.085	-.382	1.000				
GR	.166	.118	-.005	.080	.132	.130	.097	.026	-.032	1.000			
MES	.189	.065	.686	.009	.022	.059	.047	.136	-.007	-.077	1.000		
GD	-.010	.022	.124	-.066	-.092	.015	-.086	-.045	.183	-.056	.155	1.000	
DUR	.037	-.159	.055	.102	.015	.076	-.037	.032	-.343	-.022	.107	-.188	1.000

III. Empirical Results

The three-equation model was estimated using a two-stage least squares (2SLS) estimation technique which yields consistent estimates of the model's structural parameters. Those estimates are presented in Tables XIX, XX, and XXI for the price-cost margin, advertising and concentration equations respectively. All three equations were estimated using both the unadjusted and adjusted measures of vertical seller and buyer interdependence.

In the margin equation, both measures of vertical interdependence, seller and buyer, have negative relationships with price-cost margins. This is true whether the measures are unadjusted (VSI and VBI) or adjusted (AVSI and AVBI) for firm integration. This relationship is significant only for the measure of vertical buyer interdependence, however, and then primarily in the linear functional form -- equation (i).

These results are surprising for two reasons. First, the estimated relationships between price-cost margins and the measures of vertical interdependence are negative, not positive. Even though they are not significant in all of the cases, they are consistently the opposite of the positive relationship predicted by the mutual forbearance hypothesis. Secondly, the author felt that if any of the vertical relationships would be significant, it would be on the seller side and not on the buyer side. During the time period of this study, 1963, the U.S. economy was experiencing a year of moderate prosperity with excess productive

TABLE XIX

2SLS Estimates of Price-Cost Margin Equation (1)

Equation	VSI		AVSI	
	(i)	(ii)	(i)	(ii)
Constant	.1747	.1747	.1752	.1735
	(15.12)	(15.12)	(15.25)	(15.26)
AD	1.6165	1.6167	1.5979	1.5893
	(5.52)	(5.52)	(5.64)	(5.66)
CR	.0356	.0358	.0386	.0451
	(0.88)	(0.88)	(0.97)	(1.18)
KO	.1188	.1190	.1186	.1165
	(7.64)	(7.61)	(7.61)	(7.57)
MES	.1812	.1807	.1753	.1466
	(0.98)	(0.97)	(0.96)	(0.83)
GR	.2399	.2405	.2561	.2471
	(2.72)	(2.72)	(2.93)	(2.81)
GD	-.0003	-.0003	-.0003	-.0003
	(-2.88)	(-2.88)	(-3.00)	(-2.98)
VSI	-.0029	-.0035	-.0308	-.0022
	(-0.78)	(-0.49)	(-1.81)	(-0.06)
VSI^2	. . . . .	.0002	. . . . .	-.0275
		(0.11)		(-0.87)

TABLE XIX (continued)

Equation	VBI		AVBI	
	(i)	(ii)	(i)	(ii)
Constant	.1720	.1729	.1727	.1735
	(14.74)	(14.81)	(15.06)	(15.17)
AD	1.5542	1.5367	1.5684	1.5462
	(5.25)	(5.21)	(5.75)	(5.50)
CR	.0468	.0466	.0460	.0432
	(1.12)	(1.14)	(1.17)	(1.10)
KO	.1226	.1252	.1194	.1198
	(8.06)	(8.09)	(7.61)	(7.43)
MES	.1465	.1546	.1514	.1638
	(0.78)	(0.84)	(0.83)	(0.91)
GR	.2649	.2708	.2545	.2574
	(3.00)	(3.06)	(2.93)	(2.95)
GD	-.0003	-.0003	-.0003	-.0003
	(-2.47)	(-2.89)	(-3.06)	(-3.05)
VBI	-.2969	-.4992	-.3563	-.3735
	(-2.19)	(-1.97)	(-2.31)	(-0.99)
VBI^2	.....	1.4312	.....	.0838
		(0.93)		(0.06)

Figures in parentheses are t-ratios.

capacity. In this business climate it would seem that firms would be more concerned with losing sales (vertical seller interdependence) than with being foreclosed from input supplies (vertical buyer interdependence).

With respect to the other variables in the price-cost margin equation, the results are consistent with prior expectations. All of the coefficients have the expected signs and are significant at the one-percent level, except for concentration and minimum efficient scale. These two variables are highly correlated (minimum efficient scale is the main determinant of the fitted value of concentration) and may be insignificant when included in the same equation. When an F-statistic is computed testing the joint effect of these two variables it is significant at the five-percent level for all of the estimated relationships in Table XIX.

Given the significant negative relationship between price-cost margins and vertical buyer interdependence, it is of interest to examine the relative importance of this variable compared to traditional elements of market structure such as concentration and advertising. This can be done by computing the elasticity of price-cost margins with respect to these different variables, using the mean values of these variables. This elasticity is -.016 in the linear form and -.025 in the quadratic form for the unadjusted measure of vertical buyer interdependence and declines to identical values of -.007 for the adjusted measure. These figures are substantially smaller than those for·the other two variables, which range from .065-.071 for concentration and .084-.086 for advertising. Using its largest elasticity, a one hundred percent increase in vertical buyer interdependence would be associated with only a two and a half percent decrease in price-cost margins. Thus, the relationship between vertical buyer interdependence and price-cost margins, though significant, is not of a very large order of magnitude and is smaller than those between margins and other elements of market structure.

This relationship does not remain significant, however, when firm diversification is controlled for in the margin equation. In this case, the measures of vertical buyer interdependence consistently have non-significant, though still negative, relationships with price-cost margins. The coefficient for firm diversification is also consistently negative, though generally significant. These results indicate that vertical buyer interdependence has no relationship with margins once firm diversification is controlled for. Thus, the hypothesized positive relationship between vertical interdependence and price-cost margins is not supported by the regression results.

The estimates for the advertising equation are presented in Table XX and are somewhat contradictory. The unadjusted measures of vertical interdependence, both seller and buyer, have non-significant negative relationships with advertising. The adjusted measures, however, have significant positive relationships with advertising. Even though the relationships between advertising

TABLE XX

2SLS Estimates of Advertising Equation (2)

Equation	VSI		AVSI	
	(iii)	(iv)	(iii)	(iv)
Constant	-.0269	-.0271	-.0254	-.0256
	(-3.69)	(-3.72)	(-3.52)	(-3.55)
M	.0634	.0641	.0560	.0544
	(2.46)	(2.47)	(2.17)	(2.08)
CR	.0871	.0877	.0791	.0820
	(2.48)	(2.50)	(2.28)	(2.38)
CR^2	-.0842	-.0849	-.0761	-.0798
	(-2.30)	(-2.33)	(-2.11)	(-2.23)
GR	.0607	.0607	.0504	.0496
	(2.13)	(2.33)	(1.95)	(1.91)
VSI	-.0010	-.0012	.0159	.0215
	(-1.01)	(-0.60)	(3.44)	(2.02)
VSI^2	.....	.00004	.....	-.0052
		(0.09)		(-0.58)
CD	.0264	.0263	.0282	.0286
	(8.78)	(8.68)	(9.49)	(9.43)
DUR	-.0016	-.0016	-.0014	-.0014
	(-0.82)	(-0.82)	(-0.73)	(-0.75)

TABLE XX (continued)

Equation	VBI		AVBI	
	(iii)	(iv)	(iii)	(iv)
Constant	−.0266	−.0273	−.0277	−.0241
	(−3.69)	(−3.78)	(−3.83)	(−3.26)
M	.0596	.0603	.0634	.0422
	(2.38)	(2.40)	(2.45)	(1.56)
CR	.0895	.0941	.0869	.0831
	(2.62)	(2.73)	(2.49)	(2.36)
CR^2	−.0846	−.0894	−.0851	−.0776
	(−2.39)	(−2.51)	(−2.34)	(−2.12)
GR	.0655	.0663	.0540	.0509
	(2.49)	(2.52)	(2.08)	(1.95)
VBI	−.0557	−.0894	.0920	.3900
	(−1.55)	(−1.26)	(2.16)	(3.77)
VBI^2	.....	.2389	.....	−1.2662
		(0.26)		(−3.17)
CD	.0261	.0259	.0275	.0290
	(8.73)	(8.54)	(9.23)	(9.54)
DUR	−.0016	−.0016	−.0013	−.0004
	(−0.84)	(−0.85)	(−0.70)	(−0.19)

Figures in parentheses are t-ratios.

and the unadjusted measures are not significant, it is surprising that the relationship becomes positive and significant when firm integration is taken into consideration.

The coefficients for the other variables in the advertising equation all bear the expected signs and are generally significant at the five-percent level. Not surprisingly, the most significant variable is consumer demand, while the least significant variable is product durability. There is no clear-cut theoretical prediction concerning the effect of product durability on advertising intensity and this is certainly consistent with the empirical results.

To gauge the relative importance of the relationship between advertising and the adjusted measures of vertical interdependence, the elasticities of advertising with respect to these variables, as well as concentration and price-cost margins, were computed using the mean values of these variables. These elasticities are .092 in the linear case and .120 in the quadratic case for AVSI and .033 and .136 for AVBI. These elasticities are relatively small when compared to those for concentration and price-cost margins which range from .603-.682 for concentration and from .771-1.159 for margins. The adjusted measures have a significant relationship with advertising, but one which pales in importance to those between advertising and concentration and price-cost margins.

The final issue concerns the relationship between the measures

of vertical interdependence and industry concentration. Table
XXI   presents the 2SLS estimates of the concentration equation
where the measures of vertical interdependence are introduced in
conjunction with the advertising and minimum efficient scale
variables.   The only measure of vertical interdependence which is
not significantly related to concentration is the adjusted measure
of vertical buyer interdependence (AVBI).   It is, though, positively
related to concentration as are the three measures which have
significant coefficients. As expected, both advertising and
minimum efficient scale have significant positive relationships
with concentration.

It is difficult to interpret the positive relationships
between concentration and the measures of vertical interdependence.
There is not as strong a theoretical basis for these relationships
as there is for the advertising and minimum efficient scale
variables. The theoretical rationale mentioned above concerned
the possible use of predation, cross-subsidization and/or reciprocity to increase the market shares of the sample firms.   It
is not clear that the potential for these anticompetitive practices
would be captured by variables designed to measure the degree of
vertical interdependence among an industry's firms due to external
contacts.   It seems more likely that the sample firms tend to be
in concentrated industries and that this presence produces the
significant positive relationship between the measures of vertical
interdependence and concentration.

TABLE XXI

2SLS Estimates of Concentration Equation (3)

Equation	(v)	(v)	(v)	(v)
Constant	.2419 (18.79)	.2538 (21.27)	.2301 (18.44)	.2595 (21.90)
AD	1.7995 (2.86)	1.3720 (2.21)	2.0620 (3.37)	1.4096 (2.34)
MES	4.1519 (19.04)	4.1646 (19.00)	4.0643 (19.20)	4.1668 (18.87)
VSI	.0310 (3.79)	. . . . .	. . . . .	. . . . .
AVSI	. . . . .	.0971 (2.45)	. . . . .	. . . . .
VBI	. . . . .	. . . . .	1.7957 (6.71)	. . . . .
AVBI	. . . . .	. . . . .	. . . . .	.2865 (0.79)

Figures in parentheses are t-ratios.

In any event, it is possible to determine the relative importance of these relationships by computing the elasticity of concentration with respect to the different explanatory variables. As before, all elasticities were computed using the mean values of the sample variables. These elasticities are .037 and .064 for the unadjusted measures of vertical seller and buyer interdependence and .020 and .004 for the respective adjusted measures. The same figures for advertising and minimum efficient scale range from .064-.074 and .248-.257 respectively. Except for the unadjusted measure of vertical buyer interdependence, the elasticities for the measures of vertical interdependence tend to be substantially less than those for advertising and minimum efficient scale.

IV. Conclusion

The most important finding in this chapter is that vertical interdependence does not have a positive relationship with price-cost margins. This is true for both vertical buyer and seller interdependence and does not depend on the assumption about firm integration. In fact, the relationships are consistently negative and significantly so for both the unadjusted and adjusted measures of vertical buyer interdependence when they are introduced linearly in the margin equation. These last relationships become insignificant when firm diversification is controlled for, however, raising the issue of the separability of the influences of firm interdependence and firm diversification on price-cost margins.

One puzzling relationship in this chapter is the significant positive relationship between advertising intensity and the adjusted measures of vertical seller and buyer interdependence. This finding is puzzling since vertical interdependence is hypothesized to affect advertising by reducing price competition, thereby increasing non-price competition in such areas as advertising. Yet vertical interdependence does not have a positive relationship with price-cost margins, implying that price-competition is not lessened by vertical interdependence. There is no obvious ex post explanation for this significant positive relationship.

Finally, three of the four measures of vertical interdependence have a significant positive relationship with concentration. This relationship is presumably due to the sample firms producing in primarily concentrated industries.

FOOTNOTES

[1]The 1967 Input-Output tables were used instead of the 1963 tables since the author had access to those tables on computer tape. This made it possible to capture all potential vertical relationships between firms when computing the measures of vertical interdependence. If the 1963 tables had been used, the computations would have been done by hand and would have been limited to major vertical relationships. Using the tape thus permitted complete coverage of the sample firms' potential vertical interactions, though admittedly based on 1967 input-output relationships. It was the judgment of Leonard Weiss that the direct requirements coefficients were not substantially different over these two time periods.

[2]It should be noted that even though the mean value of vertical buyer interdependence is reduced by the adjustment for firm integration, the maximum value is increased from .2347 to .3226. This can occur since both the numerator and denominator of this measure are changed by the adjustment for vertical integration at the firm level. The denominator is simply the firm's total direct costs, while the numerator is a function of the firm's potential purchases of those inputs from competitors. If a firm is vertically integrated, the unadjusted measure will overstate total direct costs due to double-counting. If a plant transfers its output to another plant of the parent corporation, this output is considered a cost along with the costs incurred to produce that output. In this particular case, the change in the denominator dominated the change in the numerator and the value of the measure increased.

CHAPTER VI

Horizontal Interdependence, Vertical Interdependence

and Industry Price-Cost Margins

Firm interdependence has been hypothesized to be a function
of intermarket, as well as intramarket, contacts among an industry's
firms. Three measures of firm interdependence -- horizontal,
vertical seller and vertical buyer -- were derived and estimated to
capture the interdependence arising from the intermarket relationships among an industry's firms. In Chapters IV and V, these
measures of interdependence were introduced separately in the
three-equation model of price-cost margins. In this chapter all
three measures are introduced into the model simultaneously.
This makes it possible to estimate the total relationship between
firm interdependence and price-cost margins.

Initially, all three measures of interdependence are introduced linearly in the price-cost margin equation. The 2SLS
estimates of this specification of the margin equation are presented
in Table XXII. The equation is estimated using both the unadjusted,
equation (i), and adjusted, equation (iii), measures of vertical
seller and buyer interdependence. The horizontal measure of interdependence is HI1, the measure constructed on the assumption that
the firm had a completely inelastic demand curve. The simple
correlations between HI1 and VBI and VSI are .647 and .641
for the unadjusted measures and .257 and .454 for the adjusted

TABLE XXII

2SLS Estimates of Price-Cost Margin Equation

Equation	Unadjusted Vertical Measures		Adjusted Vertical Measures	
	(i)	(ii)	(iii)	(iv)
Constant	.1748	.1734	.1777	.1746
	(14.75)	(15.12)	(15.66)	(15.82)
AD	1.5627	1.4892	1.6428	1.4791
	(5.46)	(5.32)	(5.96)	(5.46)
CR	.0268	.0528	.0239	.0608
	(0.65)	(1.32)	(0.60)	(1.54)
KO	.1274	.1290	.1289	.1283
	(8.45)	(8.76)	(8.33)	(8.49)
MES	.2588	.1740	.2565	.1336
	(1.41)	(0.98)	(1.42)	(0.75)
GR	.2833	.3385	.2733	.3328
	(3.23)	(3.89)	(3.14)	(3.85)
GD	-.0003	-.0003	-.0003	-.0003
	(-2.64)	(-3.07)	(-3.06)	(-3.41)
HI	-.0546	-.1941	-.0409	-.1899
	(-2.32)	(-4.43)	(-2.02)	(-4.35)
HI^2	.....	.1823	.....	.1905
		(3.73)		(3.82)
VSI	.0128	.0118	-.0021	.0077
	(2.16)	(2.04)	(-0.11)	(0.40)
VBI	-.3821	-.3037	-.2771	-.2110
	(-1.75)	(-1.41)	(-1.68)	(-1.30)

Figures in parentheses are t-ratios.

measures, respectively.

The most interesting thing about these regression results is that for the first time one of the measures of interdependence has a positive relationship with price-cost margins. In equation (i), the unadjusted measure of vertical seller interdependence, VSI has a positive coefficient which is significant at the five-percent level. The other measures of interdependence, HI and VBI, both have negative relationships with margins. The coefficient for HI is significant, while that for VBI is not. The positive relationship between margins and VSI does not hold for the adjusted measure as it has a non-significant negative relationship with price-cost margins -- equation (iii). HI still has a significant negative relationship, while VBI's coefficient remains negative and non-significant.

Since the most significant relationship between the three measures and price-cost margins was the quadratic functional form with HI, this relationship was reestimated controlling for VSI and VBI. The margin equation was estimated for both the unadjusted, equation (ii), and adjusted measures of vertical interdependence, equation (iv). The results are similar to those in the linear case. HI and VBI are negatively related to price-cost margins in both equations (ii) and (iv) with HI's coefficient significant at the one-percent level in both equations. VSI is positively related to margins in both equations, but only the coefficient

for the unadjusted measure in equation (ii) is significant. It
should be noted that even after controlling for the vertical
relationships, the relationship between HI and margins, whether
linear or quadratic, is remarkably similar to those estimated
in Chapter IV.

One interesting implication of the above results is that
horizontal contacts operate to reduce price-cost margins while
vertical seller contacts tend to increase them. In order to
determine the net effect of these opposing relationships, the
mean values of these variables were multiplied by their coefficients
and compared for both the linear and quadratic cases. In the
linear case, equation (i), the resulting values are -.0059 for
HI and .0058 for VSI. Thus, the net difference is -.0001, which
increases to -.0039 if the non-significant relationship of VBI
is also included. These figures are .04 percent and 1.57 percent
of the mean value of price-cost margins, respectively. The
elasticities of price-cost margin with respect to the different
measures are of the same order of magnitude and are .023 and -.021
for VSI and VBI, and -.024 for HI.

This picture is altered in the quadratic case -- equation (ii).
Here the net effect of HI and VSI on margins is -.0135 without
VBI and -.0165 with it. These figures are 5.4 and 6.6 percent,
respectively, of the mean value of price-cost margins. This
dominant influence of HI is also reflected in the elasticities
which are now -.068, .021 and -.016 for HI, VSI and VBI respectively.

The margin elasticity of HI even approaches those of advertising, .081, and concentration, .080, in order of magnitude. In sum, the total effect of the measures is negative, in both the linear and quadratic cases, and it is modified by the positive influence of VSI.

The advertising equation was also estimated with the three measures of interdependence introduced linearly and those results are presented in Table XXIII. In equation (v), both unadjusted measures of vertical interdependence have non-significant negative relationships with advertising, while HI's coefficient is positive and significant. When the mean values of these variables are multiplied by their coefficients, their combined net effect is .0004 or 2.94 percent of the mean value of advertising. If the non-significant vertical relationships are ignored, the net effect of HI is .0018 or 12.87 percent of the mean value of advertising. This dominance of the horizontal measure is reflected in the elasticities of advertising with respect to these three measures, which are .129 for HI and -.013 and -.109 for VSI and VBI respectively.

The above picture is radically altered when the advertising equation is estimated using the adjusted measures of vertical seller and buyer interdependence -- equation (vi). The coefficients of the vertical measures become positive while that for HI becomes negative. Only the coefficient for VSI is significant, however. This dramatic change in the influence of the vertical measures is

TABLE XXIII

2SLS Estimates of Advertising Equation

Equation	Unadjusted Vertical Measures (v)	Adjusted Vertical Measures (vi)
Constant	−.0236 (−3.35)	−.0268 (−3.78)
M	.0548 (2.36)	.0554 (2.40)
CR	.0728 (2.13)	.0891 (2.55)
CR^2	−.0669 (−1.89)	−.0868 (−2.39)
GR	.0640 (2.46)	.0511 (1.99)
HI	.0161 (2.40)	−.0039 (−0.68)
VSI	−.0004 (−0.25)	.0154 (2.88)
VBI	−.1101 (−1.89)	.0457 (1.00)
CD	.0270 (9.03)	.0281 (9.41)
DUR	−.0011 (−0.59)	−.0013 (−0.69)

Figures in parentheses are t-ratios.

consistent with the results obtained in Chapter V when the advertising equation was estimated separately for VSI and VBI.
In this case, the net effect of the three measures is .0010 or
7.25 percent of the mean value of advertising. These figures are
.0012 and 8.82 percent for just VSI, the only significant measure
in the equation. Not surprisingly, the elasticity of advertising
with respect to VSI, .0891, substantially exceeds those of HI,
-.0312, and VBI, .0165, but is still minor compared to those of
concentration, .6555, and price-cost margins, 1.0127. In sum,
the net effect of these measures, in both equations, tends to be
positive and small, though there is no obvious explanation for this
relationship.

Finally, the concentration equation was estimated with all three
measures of interdependence introduced in conjunction with
advertising and minimum efficient scale. As in the price-cost
margin and advertising equations, the results are sensitive to
whether or not the vertical measures are adjusted for firm integration. With the unadjusted measures, equation (vii), HI is positive
but insignificant, while both VSI and VBI are significant but of
opposite signs. When the adjusted measures of vertical interdependence are used, equation (viii), only HI is significant
and it has a positive relationship with concentration. In both
cases, the net effect of the measures is positive and the elasticities of concentration with respect to the three measures are small
compared to those of advertising and especially minimum efficient

TABLE XXIV

2SLS Estimates of Concentration Equation

Equation	Unadjusted Vertical Measures (vii)	Adjusted Vertical Measures (viii)
Constant	.2339 (19.05)	.2431 (19.98)
AD	1.9036 (3.21)	1.3929 (2.32)
MES	4.0187 (19.05)	4.0772 (18.77)
HI	.0505 (0.93)	.1703 (3.72)
VSI	-.0326 (-2.45)	-.0332 (-0.72)
VBI	2.4329 (5.40)	-.2102 (-0.55)

Figures in parentheses are t-ratios.

scale. As noted in both Chapters IV and V, there is not a strong theoretical basis for the relationship between concentration and the measures of interdependence and more than likely it results from the sample firms producing in concentrated industries.

Two final comments should be made concerning the sensitivity of the regression results to the specification of the relationships between the endogenous variables and the measures of firm inter-dependence. First, the three-equation model was estimated using several alternative specifications of these relationships, such as quadratic functional forms and interaction variables. The regression results were always consistent with those presented above for the linear specification. Secondly, the price-cost margin equation was reestimated controlling for firm diversification. Those regression results are presented in Table XXV, where BI is a proxy for the diversified nature of an industry's firms. As defined in Chapter IV, this variable is the weighted average of the sample firms' Berry indices where the weights are the firms' market shares in the relevant industry. The unadjusted measures of vertical interdependence were used in equations (ix) and (x) and the adjusted measures in equations (xi) and (xii). Comparing Table XXV with Table XXII, it is apparent that the estimated relationships in the margin equation are not very sensitive to the inclusion of the diversification variable. The conclusions reached earlier are still valid.

In summary, the hypothesized positive relationship between

TABLE XXV

2SLS Estimates of Price-Cost Margin Equation

Equation	Unadjusted Vertical Measures		Adjusted Vertical Measures	
	(ix)	(x)	(xi)	(xii)
Constant	.1666	.1768	.1713	.1795
	(13.87)	(14.53)	(14.52)	(15.22)
AD	1.5580	1.5165	1.5745	1.5120
	(5.48)	(5.40)	(5.62)	(5.51)
CR	.0698	.0301	.0630	.0295
	(1.50)	(0.64)	(1.31)	(0.61)
KO	.1245	.1261	.1243	.1258
	(8.47)	(8.66)	(8.30)	(8.53)
MES	.1140	.2045	.1221	.1921
	(0.63)	(1.13)	(0.67)	(1.07)
GR	.2886	.3280	.2771	.3246
	(3.28)	(3.75)	(3.17)	(3.74)
GD	-.0003	-.0003	-.0003	-.0003
	(-2.77)	(-2.78)	(-3.16)	(-3.11)
HI	-.0482	-.2421	-.0391	-.2392
	(-1.78)	(-4.33)	(-1.62)	(-4.43)
HI^2	.....	.2180	.....	.2256
		(3.95)		(4.13)
VSI	.0143	.0106	-.0004	-.0010
	(2.40)	(1.77)	(-0.02)	(-0.05)
VBI	-.4341	-.3021	-.2530	-.2377
	(-2.03)	(-1.41)	(-1.51)	(-1.44)
BI	-.0225	.0537	-.0159	.0608
	(-0.60)	(1.28)	(-0.38)	(1.36)

Figures in parentheses are t-ratios.

price-cost margins and firm interdependence created by external contacts has not been supported. In fact, the evidence tends to run counter to that predicted by the mutual forbearance hypothesis. The net relationship between these three measures of interdependence and margins is negative and generally significant, though of a relatively small order of magnitude.

CHAPTER VII

Conclusions

Conglomerate mergers raise unique antitrust issues which cannot be analyzed with traditional models of the theory of the firm. This thesis examined one of those issues -- the hypothesis that conglomerate mergers reduce competition through the creation of mutual forbearance behavior. This hypothesis asserts that diversified firms will respect each other's "spheres of influence" by adopting non-aggressive behavior in those markets for fear of retaliation in other markets important to them. This hypothesis thus implies that firm behavior in one market is conditioned by firm relationships in other markets.

The objective of this thesis was twofold. First, to determine the potential for interfirm contacts among the leading firms in the American economy. This was done for a sample of 195 of the top 200 manufacturing corporations in 1963. An analysis of their manufacturing operations in 1963 indicated that an average sample firm produced in 13.6 of the 417 four-digit manufacturing S.I.C.'s and was a competitor with 76.3 of the other sample firms. This meant that an average sample firm had the potential for 2.34 horizontal and 8.83 vertical (sales) contacts with each competitor. It is difficult to place any economic meaning on these statistics, however, since there is no prior information concerning the interpretation of these numbers. They simply indicate that these leading firms have the potential for intermarket relationships with one another and that this potential undoubtedly increased as the conglomerate merger wave escalated throughout the nineteen sixties.

This information on the number of interfirm contacts was then used to accomplish the second objective of this thesis -- the empirical estimation of the relationship between the firm interdependence created by these multi-market contacts and industry price-cost margins. Measures of firm interdependence were estimated which captured both the number and relative importance of external contacts which a sample firm had with its competitors in a given market. A separate measure was constructed for each of the possible relationships which could exist between two sample firms: horizontal, vertical seller and vertical buyer. These measures were then introduced as additional explanatory variables in a three-equation model of the determinants of industry price-cost margins.

The regression results were consistently the opposite of those predicted by the mutual forbearance hypothesis. The estimated relationships between price-cost margins and the measures of firm interdependence were consistently negative and generally significantly so. This was true whether the measures of firm interdependence were introduced separately in the price-cost margin equation or were inserted in various linear and interactive combinations.

Based on these regression results, the only conclusion which seems justified is that the mutual forbearance hypothesis has not been supported. It would be both premature and unwarranted to reject the mutual forbearance hypothesis solely on the basis of these results. Such a conclusion would ignore the documented case study evidence of mutual forbearance behavior as well as the dimensions of that behavior which were not analyzed in this thesis.

This unexpected negative relationship between price-cost margins and firm interdependence does, however, invite ex post rationalizations. The natural temptation is to conclude that inter-market relationships among an industry's firms tend to increase the degree of competition in that industry. One ex post explanation offered earlier was that the logistics of arranging multi-market collusive agreements might be so complex that firms pursue independent policies instead. And this leads to more competitive behavior in the industry. This explanation is not very convincing, however, in light of recent examples which have illustrated that firms will go to enormous lengths to reach collusive agreements. The "great electrical conspiracy" was clearly a very sophisticated and complex collusive arrangement. This ex post explanation, though unlikely, does point out a major deficiency of the mutual forbearance hypothesis. Namely that it emphasizes the benefits of multi-market collusion but ignores the costs and complexities of obtaining that agreement. A more complete model of this hypothesized behavior is definitely needed.

There are two other possible explanations of this negative

relationship between the measures of firm interdependence and price-cost margins. First, the measures of firm interdependence may be capturing the influence of an omitted variable and this results in the negative relationship with margins. The most likely candidate is firm diversification which is positively correlated with the measures. There are several reasons why a negative relationship might be expected between firm diversification and margins. First, diversified firms may expand into industries which offer lower returns in order to stabilize their earnings. Secondly, the most profitable firms may also be the least diversified since investments outside the "home" industry may not equal the firm's internal rate of return. On the other hand, there are reasons why firm diversification may be positively related to margins. Diversified firms are hypothesized to have advantages over single-product firms through their capacity for cross-subsidization and reciprocal dealing. These advantages may increase entry barriers, thereby enabling those firms to earn higher profits without inviting entry. In sum, the measures of firm interdependence may be picking up the net effect of these factors in addition to the influence of mutual forbearance behavior.

This possibility was explored by reestimating the price-cost margin equation with firm diversification included as an additional explanatory variable. The relationships between margins and the measures of firm interdependence remained negative, though not significantly so in all of the cases. The results are weakened but they still do not support the mutual forbearance hypothesis.

Another possible explanation is that the deficiencies inherent in the data introduce random noise which prevents the true relationship from being estimated. Due to the level of analysis, the firm relationships tend to be more potential than actual. Even in the horizontal case, firms may produce in different regional markets and never actually meet as direct competitors. This problem is definitely more severe for the vertical relationships which are based on the input-output relationships among industries, rather than actual buyer-seller relationships among firms. These problems would, however, seem to point more toward finding no relationship rather than a significant negative one. In any event, the line-of-business reporting program of the Federal Trade Commission offers the possibility of more accurate data on firms' sales in the future, though extensive research would still be necessary to determine actual supplier-customer relationships among sample firms.

As noted above, this thesis was primarily concerned with only one dimension of mutual forbearance behavior -- pricing policy and multi-market collusion. The measures of firm interdependence were, however, also included in the advertising and concentration equations which touch on other aspects of mutual forbearance behavior. With respect to advertising, the measures of firm interdependence generally had positive relationships which were sometimes significant. This relationship was estimated in the belief that firm interdependence could conceivably operate to increase _or_ decrease the level of non-price competition. But this relationship was predicated on the assumption that firm interdependence would lessen the degree of price competition, which it did not. As a result, there is no apparent ex post explanation for this relationship.

Finally, the measures of firm interdependence were included in the concentration equation to capture the possible impact of diversified firms on this important structural variable. Diversified firms are hypothesized to have advantages over non-diversified firms such as cross-subsidization and reciprocal dealing which might enable them to expand their market shares at the expense of non-diversified rivals. The estimated relationships between concentration and these measures were generally positive and significant. Since the measures of firm interdependence were not designed for this purpose, it seems more likely that the positive relationships resulted from the sample firms producing in concentrated industries. A more appropriate analysis of this issue would be the relationship of firm diversification and the change in concentration over some time period.

One aspect of mutual forbearance behavior which can be examined with the data collected in this thesis is the relationship between firm interdependence and firm entry decisions. This is essentially an extension of the hypothesis that diversified firms will respect each other's "spheres of influence". The only difference is that collusive behavior will be reflected in entry decisions instead of pricing policies.

Finally, this thesis was undertaken because of the author's interest in the antitrust issues surrounding conglomerate mergers in general and the mutual forbearance hypothesis in particular. The results of this thesis do not support efforts to restrict con- glomerate mergers through the expansion of current case law or the enactment of new legislation. These conclusions are based solely on the issues addressed in this thesis and recognize that there might be other economic, as well as social and political, aspects of firm conglomeration which would warrant such action.

REFERENCES

W. Adams (1974), "Market Structure and Corporate Power: The
     Horizontal Dominance Hypothesis Reconsidered," Columbia Law
     Review, October, pp. 1276-1297.

B. Allen (1975), "Industrial Reciprocity: A Statistical Analysis,"
     Journal of Law and Economics, October, pp. 507-520.

C. Berry (1971), "Corporate Growth and Diversification," Journal
     of Law and Economics, October, pp. 371-384.

J. Cable (1972), "Market Structure, Advertising Policy, and Inter-
     Market Differences in Advertising Intensity," in K. Cowling,
     Market Structure and Corporate Behavior, Gray-Mills Publishing
     Limited, London, pp. 107-124.

E. Chamberlin (1956), The Theory of Monopolistic Competition,
     Harvard University Press, Cambridge, pp. 30-55.

N. Collins and L. Preston (1969), "Price-Cost Margins and Industry
     Structure," Review of Economics and Statistics, August,
     pp. 271-286.

W. Comanor and T. Wilson (1967), "Advertising, Market Structure
     and Performance," Review of Economics and Statistics, November,
     pp. 423-444.

P. Dooley (1969), "The Interlocking Directorate," American Economic
     Review, June, pp. 314-323.

R. Dorfman and P. Steiner (1954), "Optimal Advertising and Optimal
     Quality," American Economic Review, December, pp. 826-836.

C. Edwards (1955), "Conglomerate Bigness as a Source of Power,"
     in the National Bureau of Economic Conference Report, Business
     Concentration and Price Policy, Princeton University Press,
     Princeton, pp. 331-359.

W. Fellner (1949), Competition Among the Few, Knopf Press, New York.

Fortune Magazine (1963), Plant and Product Directory, 1963-1964,
     Time, Inc., New York.

L. Goldberg (1973), "The Effect of Conglomerate Mergers on
    Competition," Journal of Law and Economics, April, pp. 137-158.

_____ (1974), "Conglomerate Mergers and Concentration Ratios,"
    Review of Economics and Statistics, August, pp. 303-309.

M. Gort (1962), Diversification and Integration in American Industry,
    Princeton University Press, Princeton, New Jersey.

D. Greer (1971), "Advertising and Market Concentration," Southern
    Economic Journal, July, pp. 19-32.

J. Henderson and R. Quandt (1971), Microeconomic Theory, McGraw-
    Hill Book Company, New York.

G. Iwata (1974), "Measurement of Conjectural Variations in Oligopoly,"
    Econometrica, September, pp. 947-966.

H. Kelejian (1971), "Two-Stage Least Squares and Econometric Systems
    Linear in Parameters but Nonlinear in the Endogenous Variables,"
    Journal of the American Statistical Association, June,
    pp. 373-374.

J. Lorie and P. Halpern (1970), "Conglomerates: The Rhetoric and
    the Evidence," Journal of Law and Economics, April, pp. 147-184.

J. Markham (1955), "Survey of the Evidence and Findings on Mergers,"
    in the National Bureau of Economic Research Conference Report,
    Business Concentration and Price Policy, Princeton University
    Press, Princeton, pp. 141-212.

_____ (1973), Conglomerate Enterprise and Public Policy,
    Harvard Business School, Boston.

Moody's Investors Service (1964), Moody's Industrial Manual, 1964,
    New York.

D. Mueller (1969), "A Theory of Conglomerate Mergers," Quarterly
    Journal of Economics, November, pp. 643-659.

W. Mueller (1969), "Firm Conglomeration as a Market Structure
    Variable," American Journal of Agricultural Economics, December,
    pp. 1488-1494.

_____ (1971), "The Rising Concentration in America:
    Reciprocity, Conglomeration, and the New American 'Zaibatsu'
    System," Antitrust Law and Economics Review, Spring, pp. 15-
    50, and Summer, pp. 91-104.

W. Mueller and L. Hamm (1974), "Trends in Industrial Market Concentration, 1947 to 1970," Review of Economics and Statistics, November, pp. 511-520.

J. Narver (1967), Conglomerate Mergers and Market Competition, University of California Press, Berkeley and Los Angeles, California.

D. Needham (1969), Economic Analysis and Industrial Structure, Holt, Rinehart, and Winston, New York.

M. Nerlove and K. Arrow (1962), "Optimal Advertising Policy Under Dynamic Conditions," Economica, May, pp. 129-142.

S. Rhoades (1973), "The Effect of Diversification on Industry Profit Performance in 241 Manufacturing Industries: 1963," Review of Economics and Statistics, May, pp. 146-155.

F. Scherer (1970), Industrial Market Structure and Economic Performance, Rand McNally, Chicago.

R. Schmalensee (1972), The Economics of Advertising, North-Holland Publishing Company, Amsterdam.

M. Shubik (1960), Strategy and Market Structure, John Wiley and Sons, New York.

G. Stigler (1968), The Organization of Industry, Richard D. Irwin, Homewood, Illinois.

L. Telser (1969), "Advertising and Competition," Journal of Political Economy, December, pp. 537-562.

U.S. Bureau of the Census (1966), U.S. Census of Manufactures: 1963, U.S. Government Printing Office, Washington, D.C.

U.S. Congress, Subcommittee on Antitrust and Monopoly (1966), Concentration Ratios in Manufacturing Industry, 1963, Part I, U.S. Government Printing Office, Washington, D.C.

U.S. Department of Commerce (1974), Input-Output Structure of the U.S. Economy: 1967, Volumes 1 and 2, U.S. Government Printing Office, Washington, D.C.

U.S. Federal Trade Commission (1969), Economic Report on Corporate Mergers, Government Printing Office, Washington, D.C.

U.S. Federal Trade Commission (1972), Conglomerate Merger Performance: An Empirical Analysis of Nine Corporations, Government Printing Office, Washington, D.C.

L. Weiss (1963), "Factors in Changing Concentration," Review of Economics and Statistics, February, pp. 70-77.

_____ (1971), "Quantitative Studies in Industrial Organization," in M. Intriligator, Frontiers of Quantitative Economics, North-Holland Publishing Company, Amsterdam, pp. 362-411.

_____ (1975), "The Concentration-Profits Relationship and Anti-trust," unpublished manuscript.

O. Williamson (1963a), "Selling Expense as a Barrier to Entry," Quarterly Journal of Economics, February, pp. 112-128.

_____ (1963b), "Managerial Discretion and Business Behavior," American Economic Review, December, pp. 1032-1057.

O. Williamson and N. Bhargava (1972), "Assessing and Classifying the Internal Structure and Control Apparatus of the Modern Corporation," in K. Cowling, Market Structure and Corporate Behavior, Gray-Mills Publishing Limited, London, pp. 125-148.

For Product Safety Concerns and Information please contact our EU
representative GPSR@taylorandfrancis.com Taylor & Francis Verlag GmbH,
Kaufingerstraße 24, 80331 München, Germany

Printed and bound by CPI Group (UK) Ltd, Croydon, CR0 4YY

08/05/2025

01864445-0003